I0054220

Retirement Terms

Financial Education Is Your Best Investment

Published February 11, 2020

Revision 2.2

Financial Terms Dictionary

Copyright And Trademark Notices

Limits of Liability and Disclaimer of Warranties

The materials in this book are provided "as is" and without warranties of any kind either express or implied. The Author disclaims all warranties, express or implied, including, but not limited to, implied warranties of merchant-ability and fitness for a particular purpose.

The Author does not warrant that defects will be corrected, or that that the site or the server that makes this eBook available are free of viruses or other harmful components. The Author does not warrant or make any representations regarding the use or the results of the use of the materials in this book in terms of their correctness, accuracy, reliability, or otherwise. Applicable law may not allow the exclusion of implied warranties, so the above exclusion may not apply to you.

Under no circumstances, including, but not limited to, negligence, shall the Author be liable for any special or consequential damages that result from the use of, or the inability to use this eBook, even if the Author or his authorized representative has been advised of the possibility of such damages.

Applicable law may not allow the limitation or exclusion of liability or incidental or consequential damages, so the above limitation or exclusion may not apply to you. In no event shall the Author's total liability to you for all damages, losses, and causes of action (whether in contract, tort, including but not limited to, negligence or otherwise) exceed the amount paid by you, if any, for this eBook.

Facts and information are believed to be accurate at the time they were placed in this book. All data provided in this book is to be used for information purposes only. The information contained within is not intended to provide specific legal, financial or tax advice, or any other advice whatsoever, for any individual or company and should not be relied upon in that regard. The services described are only offered in jurisdictions where they may be legally offered. Information provided is not all-inclusive and is limited to information that is made available and such information should not be relied upon as all-inclusive or accurate.

You are advised to do your own due diligence when it comes to making business decisions and should use caution and seek the advice of qualified professionals. You should check with your accountant, lawyer, or professional advisor, before acting on this or any information. You may not consider any examples, documents, or other content in this eBook or otherwise provided by the Author to be the equivalent of professional advice.

The Author assumes no responsibility for any losses or damages resulting from your use of any link, information, or opportunity contained in this book or within any other information disclosed by the author in any form whatsoever.

About the Author

Thomas Herold is a successful entrepreneur, mediator, author, and personal development coach. He published over 35 books with over 200,000 copies distributed worldwide and the founder of seven online businesses.

For over ten years Thomas Herold has studied the monetary system and has experienced some profound insights on how money and wealth are related. After three years of successful investing in silver, he released 'Building Wealth with Silver - How to Profit From The Biggest Wealth Transfer in History' in 2012. One of the first books that illustrate in a remarkable, simple way the monetary system and its consequences.

He is the founder and CEO of the 'Financial Terms Dictionary' book series and website, which explains in detail and comprehensive form over 1000 financial terms. In his financial book series, he informs in detail and with practical examples all aspects of the financial sector. His educational materials are designed to help people get started with financial education.

In his 2018 released book 'The Money Deception', Mr. Herold provides the most sophisticated insight and shocking details about the current monetary system. Never before has the massive manipulation of money caused so much economic inequality in the world. In spite of these frightening facts, 'The Money Deception' also provides remarkable and simple solutions to create abundance for all people, and it's a must-read if you want to survive the global monetary transformation that's underway right now.

In 2019 he released an entirely new financial book series explaining in detail and with practical examples over 1000 financial terms. The 'Herold Financial IQ Series' contains currently of 16 titles covering every category of the financial market.

His latest book "High Credit Score Secrets" offers the most effective strategies to boost the average credit score from as low as 450 points to over 810. It teaches the tactics to build excellent credit, repair credit, monitor credit and how to guard that good score for a lifetime. It reached bestseller status in 2020 in three categories.

For more information please visit the author's websites:

High Credit Score Secrets - The Smart Raise & Repair Guide to Excellent Credit
https://highcreditscoresecrets.com

The Money Deception - What Banks & Government Don't Want You to Know
https://www.moneydeception.com

The Herold Financial IQ Series - Financial Education Is Your Best Investment
https://www.financial-dictionary.com

The Online Financial Dictionary - Over 1000 Terms Explained
https://www.financial-dictionary.info

Please Leave Your Review on Amazon

This book and the Financial IQ Series are self-published and the author does not have a contract with one of the five largest publishers, which are able to support the author's work with advertising. If you like this book, please consider leaving a solid 4 or 5-star review on Amazon.

Herold Financial IQ Series on Amazon

Table Of Contents

1035 Exchange

A 1035 Exchange is an exchange process that permits individuals to replace their existing life insurance policy or annuity contract with a similar new contract or policy. Thanks to a provision in the tax code, this can be affected without suffering any negative tax repercussions as part of the trade off exchange. The Internal Revenue Service permits those who hold these kinds of contracts to update their old policies and annuities with those more modern ones that include better benefits, superior investment choices, and lower fees.

The 1035 Exchange is also called a Section 1035 Exchange after the tax code section for which it is named. It literally permits policyholders to transfer their funds out of an endowment, life insurance policy, or annuity into a newer similar vehicle. The way it works is to allow holders to defer their gains. When all of the received proceeds of the original contract become transferred to the newer contract (as there are simultaneously not any loans outstanding on the prior policy), no tax becomes due at point of exchange. Should these proceeds be received and not exchanged according to the 1035 Exchange rules, then all gains obtained out of the first contract become taxable like ordinary income, and not as capital gains.

Gains do not refer to all money received. Instead they are the result of subtracting the gross cash value from the premium tax basis. This basis refers to the original dollar amount put into the contract itself minus the premiums paid for extra benefits or any distributions which qualify as tax free.

In order for this 1035 Exchange to make sense, it has to benefit the policy holder either economically or personally. It is also important for holders to never terminate their in place insurance policies until the newer policy has been fully issued and becomes effective. The holders need to contemplate any health changes since the original policy started. It might cost extra premiums in order for the newer policy to cover them. They might even receive a denial of coverage if the changes in health are too drastic. Similarly, if the holder is well advanced in age, the premium rate may increase.

Some policies also have surrender charges that must be considered. There may be different guarantees, provisions, and interest crediting in the newer policy as well. Most importantly, benefits of the newer policy have to be carefully reviewed. These may change negatively in some cases.

There are rare cases where simply surrendering an existing insurance policy or annuity is more advantageous than engaging in a 1035 Exchange. These primarily occur when the existing contract offers no gain. Sometimes outstanding loans on the initial policy also decrease the benefits of an exchange. In other cases, the original policy may have a "market rate adjustment" type of provision. This would cause the exchange proceeds to be less than those offered in a surrender.

It is usually the case that such a 1035 Exchange will be slower and more involved than simply surrendering the holder's original policy. It can even require a few months much of the time. This is why the conditions that affect the practicality of the exchange include financial conditions of the initial policy carrier, the country's economic climate at the time, and the intentions of the policy holder.

The IRS only deems certain exchanges to be considered "like kind" and allowable. These include life insurance for life insurance, life insurance for non-qualified annuity, life insurance for endowment, endowment for non-qualified annuity, endowment for endowment, and non-qualified annuity for non-qualified annuity. They also will allow multiple numbers of existing contracts to be changed into a single newer contract. It does not work in reverse. A single existing contract can not be exchanged in for multiple newer contracts, per the IRS rules and regulations.

401(k) Plan

401k retirement plans are specific kinds of accounts that the government established to help individuals to plan and save for retirement. Individuals fund these accounts using pre-taxed dollars from payrolls.

People invest money in these accounts into several different types of investments. These include stocks, mutual funds, and bonds. Gains earned in the account include dividends, capital gains, and interest. These gains do not get taxed until the owners withdraw the funds.

The name of the 401k comes from the portion of Internal Revenue Service Code which pertains to it. This vehicle for saving for retirement began in 1981 when an act of Congress created it.

There are a number of benefits to 401k accounts that recommend them to individuals. Five of these include tax benefits, flexibility of investments, employer matching programs, loan abilities, and portability.

The advantageous tax benefits are one of the main reasons that 401k plans are so popular. Money contributed does not become taxable until individuals withdraw it. Similarly gains accrued in the account are also tax-deferred. Over several decades, this makes a significant difference in the amount of money that people can save.

Investments that the IRS allows in these 401k retirement plans provide some flexibility. Those who do not want to take on much risk can choose to put more of their funds into shorter term bonds which are lower risk. Others who are more concerned with developing wealth over the long term can put a larger percentage of the money into equities like stocks and mutual funds. Company stock can also be acquired at a discount with many employers.

A tremendous edge that these 401k retirement plans provide their owners is the employer match feature. A great number of employers match their employees' contributions as a company benefit. This is done on a percentage basis. Newer employees may receive a 25% of contributions match, while employees who have been at a company longer may receive 50% or even 100% matches. Matches are only made on a certain maximum percentage of income that an employee contributes. This is the closest thing to free money a person can obtain at work.

Loan abilities from 401k retirements are a helpful feature for individuals in times of need. When people find themselves needing money with no other place to turn, the government permits them to obtain 401k loans from the plan. The plan administrator has to approve it as well. Loans from 401k plans are not taxed or penalized so long as they are repaid according to the repayment schedule and terms.

There are no restrictions on the uses of such loans. Some employers have minimum amounts that can be borrowed of $1,000 and a maximum number of loans an employee can take at a time. Sometimes employees will have to get their spouse's written consent before the company will issue the loan.

There are limits on the amount of a balance that can be borrowed. This is typically as much as 50% of the vested balance to no more than $50,000. When an employer will not allow an employee to take out a loan against the plan, hardship withdrawals can be requested. These are taxed and also penalized at a 10% rate.

Portability means the 401k retirement plan can go with the employees as they change jobs. Investors have four different choices for their 401k plan when they move to another company. They can choose to leave the plan with the old employer and pay any administration fees for the account staying there. They might instead do a rollover of their account to the new employer's 401k retirement plan.

A third option is to convert the 401k retirement plan into an Individual Retirement Account. Finally they might decide to close the 401k and receive the proceeds in cash. This would mean all money would be subject to taxes and the 10% penalty fee.

403(b) Plan

403(b) plans were created for employees of schools, churches, and tax exempt organizations. Individuals who are eligible may establish and maintain their own 403(b) accounts. Their employers can and often do make contributions to the employees' accounts. Individuals are able to open one of three different types of 403(b)s.

The first is an annuity plan that an insurance company establishes. These types of plans are sometimes called TDAs tax deferred annuities or TSAs tax sheltered annuities. A second plan type is an account which a retirement custodian offers and manages. With these 403(b)s, the account holders may only choose from mutual funds and regulated investment companies that the custodian allows. The final type is a retirement income account. These accounts accept a combination of mutual funds or annuities for the investment choices.

Employers have some control over these accounts. They are able to decide which financial institution will hold the employees' 403(b) accounts. This determines the kind of plan that the employees are able to set up and fund. Employers receive several advantages from choosing to offer a 403(b).

The benefits which they get to offer their employees are worthwhile. This helps to ensure valuable employees stay with the organization. They also enjoy sharing the funding costs between themselves and their employees. Employers may also choose for the 403(b) to only accept employee contributions if they do not wish to participate financially in the account.

Employees also experience several benefits from these types of retirement vehicles. They may contribute tax deferred dollars from their income. They may also contribute taxed dollars to the accounts. In these Roth 403(b)s, all of their earnings accrue tax free for the entire life of the account. Deferred tax payments until retirement typically allow for the employees to pay fewer taxes as they are often in a more advantageous tax bracket at retirement point. Employees may also obtain loans from their 403(b) accounts as they need them.

A variety of non profit organizations may choose to establish such a 403(b) plan for their employees. This includes any 501(c)(3) tax exempt organization, co-op hospital service organizations, public school systems, ministers at churches, Native American public school systems, and (USUHS) Uniformed Services for the University of the Health Sciences.

Such 403(b) plans can obtain a variety of contribution types. Employees may have elective deferral contributions taken out of each paycheck. These are taken out in a pretax dollars arrangement. Employees also have the ability to contribute taxed dollars to the accounts. They have these deducted from their payrolls as well.

Employers may also choose to make contributions which are either discretionary or fixed amounts as they desire. Employees and employers may make contributions to Roth 403(b) accounts. These 403(b) accounts may also receive any combination of the previously mentioned contribution types, which demonstrates their flexibility.

Employees have generous annual contribution limits with these plans. In 2016, they may contribute up to $18,000 (or $24,000 if they are over 50 years old and catching up on contributions for retirement). For 2016, employers may also deposit as much as $53,000 (up to 100% of the employee compensation) as an annual contribution.

Regarding distributions, the rules are comparable to the other types of retirement savings vehicles. Distributions of deferred taxed dollars become taxable like regular income when the employee receives them. If these are taken before the employee turns 59 ½, then the withdrawn dollars are assessed the standard 10% penalty for early withdrawals. There are some exceptions to this penalty for which an employee may qualify. One of these exceptions is if the employee terminates the job even before reaching the age of retirement.

408(k) Plan

The 408(k) Plan is a retirement plan that employers set up to assist their employees in saving money for their post working years. It is named for the section of the IRS code that describes these accounts. Though there are some distinctions, a 408(k) Plan is actually a simpler version of the ever popular 401(k) plan.

These 408(k)'s are intended for smaller companies which employ fewer than 25 staff. Self employed individuals are also able to take advantage of these plans. SEP Simplified Employee Pensions are another name for the 408(k)'s.

These plans are practical and useful for workers because they are able to contribute dollars that have not yet been taxed. In addition to helping them save for retirement, it lowers their net incomes for the tax year in question. This can reduce the tax bracket into which the employees fall. It leads to lower taxes for the individuals who contribute. The deposits do not become taxable as income until the point where the employees take their money back in the form of distributions.

Employers are also able to contribute funds to the account on behalf of the employees and in their names. The employer contributions are similarly tax deductible. Besides providing the employer with a nice benefit to offer their workers, it saves them on their annual company tax bill as well. Though these accounts are set up by employers, they remain in the name of the employees and for their sole benefits.

408(k) plans share many features with their 401(k) cousins. The 408(k)'s are somewhat simpler to understand, set up, and utilize. Both plans have yearly maximum contribution limits. With these plans, the employees also do not pay any taxes for contributions which the employer makes in the account. Both accounts are also tax deferred.

Taxes will only become due when the employee takes distributions at the retirement age starting at 59 and a half. Until that point, none of the money they contribute will be treated like income. There are some limitations and restrictions on these kinds of accounts. They can be utilized by self employed individuals and smaller companies. They may not be set up by larger companies which count more than 25 employees.

Employees can not contribute more than the maximum annual limit to these accounts. If they do, the surplus dollars will be treated as income, taxed, and also penalized by 10%. Money which an employee takes out early before retirement age is also subject to taxes and 10% penalties.

There is an exception to this early withdrawal rule. If an employee feels the financial need, he or she is allowed to take money back without penalties on a loan basis only. 408(k) plans do allow for such loans, provided that they are repaid. The money must be paid back to the account according to a payment schedule set up with the plan administrator. In the even that it is not put back, the loan amount becomes treated as an early withdrawal distribution. In this case, the full tax and 10% penalty amount will apply to the total loan principle.

The maximum contribution amounts to the 408(k) Plans vary by year. The IRS increases the limits from time to time to compensate for projected inflation. When employees reach 50, they are allowed to increase their contributions per year to an IRS allowed larger dollar amount. This is to help them to catch up on any contributions which they may have missed out on over the years.

412(i) Plan

412(i) Plans are pension plans that are classified as qualified defined benefit arrangements. They were established by the IRS for small companies and self employed business owners to have a way to save for their retirement and those of their employees. Employers fund these plans with only fixed annuities or both annuities and permanent life insurance.

For the 412(i) Plans to be qualified and legal, they must meet the standards for these kinds of plans. This includes non discrimination rules and eligibility requirements. All employees of the firm who are over 20 years old must be included if they have worked there for at least a year.

These plans have become more popular with time. This is in part because employers fund them with guaranteed investments. When they contribute fixed annuities, the retirement benefits are figured by utilizing the annuity's guaranteed purchase rate. If life insurance contracts are contributed, benefits are based on the guaranteed cash accumulation of the policies. One advantage this gives the small business owner is the ability to fund contributions in dollar amounts which are larger than the amounts that competing qualified plans allow. The contributions they make are also tax deductible. This reduces the tax burden for the contribution year.

There are several benefits that these plans feature. The monthly benefit for the account holder is guaranteed. They create large income tax deductions for the benefits of the employers. Besides this these plans offer significant death benefits for the account holders. These mean that these 412(i) Plans provide small businesses with an attractive package for obtaining and keeping important talent. They also help the small company's employees who can count on the guaranteed and fixed benefits at retirement.

412(i) Plans are special because they do not have to live up to complicated rules for funding them adequately. There are also no yearly actuarial requirements to certify that the plan is properly funded. The guaranteed parts of the fixed annuities and life insurance vehicles ensure that these defined benefit plans will be solvent. The only requirement to ensure that this happens is for the employer to continuously pay the annual policy or annuity premiums.

The life insurance company provides all of the guarantees that the plan requires. One important feature of these and other defined benefit plans is that they do not always allow account holders to take loans out of the plan. The Pension Protection Act of 2006 set out many of the standards for these plans and also provided an alternative number of 412(e)(3) for them.

If annuity policies yield a greater amount of dividends or interest than is guaranteed, this benefits the employer. The plan rules stipulate that the extra payments credit against upcoming premiums. If the life insurance contract offers dividends, these are also applied against premiums in the future. They do not go to the account holder, but always to reduce the premiums of the 412(i) Plans.

There are important reasons that employers choose to include a contract of life insurance in such 412(i) Plans. They offer fully tax deductible ways of giving the small business owner and employees death benefits. When the beneficiary receives this benefit, the face value minus the cash value (of the policy's death benefit) distributes as a tax free income. This life insurance contained within the plan gives the account holders valuable estate liquidity that it will likely need after they have passed away.

The insurance companies which offer the annuity contract or the insurance policy for the plan do not usually provide administration for the 412(i) Plans. This service is typically supplied by IRS approved third party administrators.

457(b) Plan

A 457(b) plan is a retirement savings vehicle. It derives its name from the Internal Revenue Service code that regulates the plans in its section 457(b). Many times this retirement account name is simply shortened to 457 Plan.

There are many similarities between these 457 Plans and tax deferred, employer provided retirement vehicles including 403(b) and 401(k) plans. All of these retirement vehicles are defined contribution plans. People who participate in these 457 Plans set up payroll deductions so that a portion of their income is put into this investment account that is tax free.

The government established these 457 Plans in 1978. They were set up to be another defined contribution account that would help two particular kinds of employers. They are intended for both government employers and non government employers which are tax exempt as with hospitals and charities.

Despite this fact, a few different rules apply for the government plans as opposed to the non government plans. The principle difference revolves around funding. Government 457 Plans have to be funded by the employer in question. The non government 457 Plans are practically all funded by employees. The vast majority of 457(b) plans that private not for profit companies use they only offer to well paid employees usually in upper level management.

With 457 Plans, there must be both a plan administrator and a plan provider. Each plan provides its own limited choices for investment options which are particular to the plan.

Rollover rules are different for these 457 Plans as well. The non government versions can not be transferred over to qualified retirement plans which include IRA and 401(k)s. Instead they can only be rolled over to other tax exempt 457 Plans. The rules are different with government sponsored employer plans. These may be transferred into another employer's 401(k), 403(b), or 457(b) plan as well as to an IRA account. The new plan must permit account holders to make such transfers.

Withdrawals are easier for government sponsored plans as well. Individuals may do early withdrawals before they reach the 59 ½ year old age of retirement and not have to suffer the 10% early withdrawal penalty. The full withdrawn amount would be taxed as regular income. Employees who are switching jobs may also keep the money where it is assuming the plan permits this.

Rollover rules on 457(b) plans are pretty standard. If funds are dispersed to the account owner, he or she has a maximum of 60 days to finish the rollover process. Beyond this time, the IRS considers this money to have been distributed and to be taxable. Owners are also restricted to doing a single rollover in a calendar year with these retirement vehicles.

The date on which the owners receive their 457 Plan distribution is when the one year rule commences. While the money is in the 60 day process of being rolled over, it may not be invested. Direct rollovers avoid the dangers of the 60 day rule. An account holder never obtains a distribution check (as with indirect rollovers) in this type of transfer. Instead, the plan provider will directly transfer all money to the new IRA or retirement plan.

Investment choices in 457 Plans are more limited than with Self Directed IRAs or Solo 401(k) plans. The plan provider will restrict choices to ones that fit their plan. If they permit them, owners may invest their funds in individual bonds and stocks, fixed or indexed annuities, exchange traded funds, and mutual funds.

Gold bullion can not be purchased by these plans. Paper gold investments such as stocks of gold mining firms, mutual funds containing gold mining companies, or gold ETFs like GLD and mining ETFs may be purchased instead.

American International Group (AIG)

American International Group is one of the largest insurance companies in the world. It boasts over 90 million customers living in over 100 countries around the globe. The company has provided risk management and insurance services for customers for almost a hundred years.

Today the company is changing to try to meet their clients' needs better. They are simplifying the corporate structure to be able to work more directly with their customers, to provide value and help quicker and with greater efficiency, and to offer better transparency. They are striving for greater focus, leaner operations, and higher profits.

AIG proves to be the largest commercial insurance company for both the United States and Canada. They rank as biggest nonlife insurance operation in the world based on market capitalization. Fully 98% of Fortune 500 companies, 90% of Fortune Global 500 corporations, and 96% of Fortune 1000 Companies carry their insurance products or services.

American International Group began life as the brain child and insurance project of American Cornelius Vander Starr in 1919. He established it as the AAU American Asiatic Underwriters general insurance company in Shanghai at this time. This outfit expanded throughout China and then around the world.

Each new culture and market they encountered helped them to broaden their concept of risk and the means of helping to manage it for their customers. As World War II was breaking out, the company wisely relocated its headquarters from Shanghai in China to New York City. The company continued to expand successfully throughout Latin America, Asia, Africa, and Europe through 2008.

When the financial crisis erupted in the United States in 2008, the U.S. government had to bail out the company to save it from collapse. Edward M. Liddy was appointed as Chairman of AIG in order to navigate it through the chaotic and troubled operating environment and company era. By 2012, AIG had succeeded in restructuring the company. They also repaid all of the aid and loans from the U.S. government with profits that year, relaunched their damaged brand, and restored their reputation.

AIG boasts a number of impressive accomplishments in the intervening years since emerging from the financial crisis. They have once again become a market leader for aiding families in safeguarding their financial futures. They are the number one ranked fixed rate deferred annuity providers. AIG is among the biggest sellers of group retirement plans as well. In a number of countries throughout the globe, the outfit is a personal insurance policy leader. Nearly half of the wealthiest Americans (as measured by the Forbes 400 Richest Americans) choose AIG for their nonlife insurance needs.

AIG has won and continues to win numerous awards for their performance, service, and products. In 2016 they were honored with the top spot at the Business Insurance Innovation Awards. This is a position that they or one of their companies have successfully held for 7 years in a row. They won three honors at the Travvy Awards in 2016. They also earned a third year in a row place on the Diversity Inc. 25 Noteworthy Companies for Diversity.

AIG is also pioneering technology and data science techniques for helping to ensure their clients are better informed and safer. They have an unrivaled amount of information and expertise that they utilize to provide insights into a wide variety of sectors around the globe. These enable them to help stop losses and reap better results for the company and its customers. AIG routinely shares the exploration results of this information with governments, researchers, non government organizations, and experts in various fields.

Annuity

An annuity is an investment contract that an insurance company sells to individuals. This agreement promises that it will make a regular series and dollar amount of payments to the buyer. This can be either for the rest of his or her life or for a set amount of time. The payments out are typically made after the individual retires.

Annuities have a long past that began in the Roman Empire. Roman citizens could purchase annual contracts from the Roman Emperor. The empire would then make annual payments to the citizens for the remainder of their lives. European governments revived the sale of annuities in the 1600s. They sold lump sum contracts to investors to help pay for expensive wars.

These investors also received a number of prearranged payments back from the governments that sold them. Annuities in America started as a way to support church ministries. 1912 saw the first annuity contract that was offered to the general American public by a Pennsylvania life insurance firm. These contracts continued to evolve and grow throughout the 1950s until they became commonplace in the 1980s.

Annuities offer certain tax advantages to their owners. Annuity holders only pay taxes on their contributions when they begin to take withdrawals or distributions from the funds. Every annuity contract is tax deferred. This signifies that investment earnings in such annuity accounts continue to grow tax deferred until the owners withdraw them. This also means that annuity earnings may not be taken out without paying a penalty until the owner reaches the set age of 59 1/2.

There are two general types of annuities contracts. Fixed annuities pledge to provide a guaranteed payment amount. Variable annuities do not make this guarantee. They do offer the possibility of earning higher returns in the variable annuity. Experts consider either type of annuity to be a safe but low yielding investment vehicle.

Annuities have a specific purpose. Companies developed them in order to insure the owner against the possibility of living longer than his or her retirement income. This is known as superannuation. The idea behind annuities is to help offset this risk of outliving retirement funds.

Annuities are popular with conservative investors because they continue to make payments until the holder dies. Even when the payments surpass the amount that remains in the annuity, the payments continue to be made. They are always counted as retirement savings vehicles.

The two phases of annuities are the accumulation and the distribution periods. During the accumulation phase, owners do one of two things. They can make a large lump sum payment into the annuity. They may also make regular payments into the contract. If the owner dies in this accumulation period, the heirs are given the amount of money that the owner paid into the annuity contract. Taxes owed would include estate taxes and regular income taxes.

When the owner reaches the retirement age, annuitization happens and distribution begins. At this point, the accumulated amounts convert into annuity units. The owner is changing the lump sum amount in the contract for the guaranteed series of payments. At this point he or she no longer has access to the large single amount in the account. The guaranteed income for life begins in this distribution phase.

Owners can receive their benefits as one of several options. Straight Life contracts pay calculated sums that are only based on the owner's life expectancy. These payments stop when the owner dies even if a lesser amount than the contract value is distributed. Life with Period Certain option makes payments for a minimum amount of time up to the death of the owner. Joint Life option pays benefits until both owners have died. Joint Life with Period Certain option gives payments for a guaranteed minimum amount of time until both owners have died.

Asset Classes

Asset classes are different groups of securities which demonstrate characteristics in common, are governed by similar regulations and laws, and behave similarly in the markets. There are five principle classes which include equities (stocks), fixed income (bonds), money market instruments (cash equivalent), commodities (like gold and oil), and real estate (including land, houses, and commercial buildings), as well as some other less common alternative classes of assets.

Many times these different classes of assets are intermingled by financial advisors and analysts. They like these different types of investment vehicles to diversify portfolios more effectively and efficiently. Every asset class is anticipated to provide differing levels and types of risks versus returns among its investment characteristics. They also are supposed to perform differently in any given investment climate. Those investors who seek out the highest possible returns typically do this by lowering their overall portfolio risk by performing diversification of asset classes.

Financial professionals typically focus their clients on the different asset classes as a means of steering them into proper and effective diversification of their investment or retirement portfolios. The various classes of assets possess differing amounts and types of risk as well as varying cash flows. By purchasing into several of the competing asset classes, investors make certain they obtain a proper level of diversification in their investment choices. The importance of diversification can not be overstated. This is because all financial professionals in the know understand that it lowers risk while maximizing the opportunities to earn the highest possible return.

There are a variety of different types of investment strategies available to investors today. They might be associated with value, growth, income, or a combination of some or all of these factors. Each of them works to categorize and label the various investment options per a particular grouping of investment criteria.

There are many analysts who prefer to tie traditional valuation metrics like price to earnings ratios (PE ratios) or growth in earnings per share (EPS) to the investment selection criteria. Still different analysts feel like performance is less of a priority while asset type and allocation are more critical. They know that investments which are in the identical class of assets will possess similar cash flows, returns, and risks.

The most liquid of these various asset classes prove to be equities, fixed income securities, cash- like instruments, and commodities. This also makes them the most frequently quoted, traded, and recommended classes of assets available today. Other asset classes are considered to be more alternative such as real estate, stamps, coins, and artwork, all of which are tradable forms of collectibles. There are also investment choices such as venture capital funds, crowd sourcing, hedge funds, and bitcoin, which are considered to be even more alternative and mostly for sophisticated investors. In general, the rule is that the more alternative the investment turns out to be, the less liquidity it actually possesses.

Some of these investments, such as hedge funds, venture capital funds, and crowd sourcing can take years to exit from, if investors are able to withdraw from the investment at all. Lower liquidity does not necessarily correlate to lower return potential though. It only means that it may be a while before holders are able to find a willing buyer to sell the investments to so they can cash out of the investment.

Many of the most alternative types of investments have boasted among the highest returns over the decades, sometimes significantly better returns than the most popular two asset classes of stocks and bonds. In order to get around this lack of liquidity and often enormous investment capital requirement, many investors choose to utilize REITS. Real Estate Investment Trusts provide greater liquidity while still participating in price appreciation of the real estate asset class.

Asset Protection

Asset Protection and planning refers to strategies and practices for protecting personal wealth. It happens through deliberate and involved planning processes that safeguard individuals' assets from the potential claims of any creditors. Both businesses and individuals alike can employ these specific techniques to reduce the ability of creditors to seize personal or business property within the legal boundaries of creditor debtor law.

What makes Asset Protection so powerful is that it is able to insulate a variety of assets and all legally. It does not require any of the shady or illegal activities inherent in concealing assets, illegal money transferring, bankruptcy fraud, or tax evasion. The asset experts will warn their clients that efficient protection of assets starts in advance of a liability, incident, or claim occurring. The reason is that it is generally over late to begin arranging such protection afterward. There are a wide variety of normal means for protecting such personal or business assets. Among the most popular are family limited partnerships, accounts receivable financing, and asset protection trusts.

In the heavily litigious society of the United States, Asset Protection involves protecting property from those who might win a judgment in court. There are a variety of lawsuits that could threaten a person's or business' assets. Among these are car accident claims, unintentional negligent acts, and even foreclosure on property lawsuits where the mortgage is no longer paid. The ultimate goal in Asset Protection is to take any nonexempt from creditors assets and move them to a position where they become exempt assets beyond the reach of any claims of the various creditors.

Asset Protection which an individual or business does when a lawsuit is already underway or even imminent to be filed will likely be reversed by the courts. This way they can seize the hidden assets that were deliberately transferred to protect them from an imminent court case judgment. This is the ultimate reason why effective protection of assets has to start well in advance of the first hints of litigious activity or creditor claims.

Two principal goals must be combined in order to effectively construct an efficient and ironclad Asset Protection plan. These include achieving both long term and short term goals and reaching estate planning goals. The financial goals component involves clearly understanding present and future income sources, the amount of resources needed for retirement, and any resources which will remain to leave to any heirs via estate planning. This helps people to come up with highly detailed financial plans.

After this has been done, individuals will want to examine carefully any present assets to decide if they are effectively exempted from any and all sundry creditors. The ones that are not should be clearly repositioned so that they are exempt. This also involves planning to position future assets so that they are similarly effectively protected.

The next step is to come up with a complete and all inclusive estate plan. It should encompass all forms of asset protection and relevant planning via advanced techniques of estate planning. Among these are irrevocable trusts for the individuals, their children, spouses, and beneficiaries as well as family limited liability companies.

The most common mistake that people or businesses make with this Asset Protection planning is waiting until it is too late to safeguard the assets. The other mistake is assuming that such planning can be done rapidly or as a short term fix for a longer term problem. Protecting assets is ultimately longer term planning that must be done carefully and ahead of potential creditor claims on assets or pending lawsuits.

Capital Appreciation

Capital appreciation refers to the increase in an asset's value. This gain is based on the increase in the market price of the asset. It primarily happens as the asset which an investor backed goes for a greater market price than the investor first paid for the asset in question. The part of the asset which is considered to be capital appreciating covers the entire market value which exceeds the cost basis, or original amount invested.

There are two principle sources of returns on investment. The largest of these is typically the capital appreciating component of the return. The other return source is from dividends or interest income. The total return of an investment results from the inclusion of both the appreciation of capital and the dividend return or interest income.

There are a wide variety of reasons why capital appreciation can occur in the first place. These differ from one asset class or market to the next, but the idea is the same. With financial assets like stocks or hard assets such as real estate, this can occur similarly.

Examples of this appreciation of capital abound. If a stock investor buys shares for $20 a piece while the stock provides a yearly dividend of $2, then the dividend yield is ten percent. A year after this, if the stock is trading at $30 and the investor obtained the $2 dividend, then the investor has enjoyed a return of $10 in capital appreciating since the stock increased from $20 to $30. The percent return of the stock price increase amounts to a capital appreciating level of 50 percent. With the $2 dividend return, the dividend yield is another ten percent. That makes the combined capital appreciation between the stock price increase and the dividend payout $12, or 60 percent. This stunning total return would please most any investor in the world.

A variety of different causes can lead to this appreciation of capital for a given asset. A generally rising trend can support the prices of the investment. These can come from such macroeconomic factors as impressive GDP growth or accommodative policies of the Federal Reserve in lowering their benchmark interest rates. It might also be something more basic having to do with the company that issued the stock itself. Stock prices could rise when the firm is outperforming the prior expectations of analysts. The real estate value of a house or other property could increase because it has good proximity to upcoming new developments like major roads, shopping centers, or good schools.

Mutual funds are another investment example which seeks out capital appreciation. The funds hunt for investments which will likely increase in value because of their undervalued but solid fundamentals or because they have earnings which outperform analysts' expectations. It is true that such investments often entail larger risks than those alternatives picked for income generation or preservation of capital, as with municipal bonds, government bonds, or high dividend paying stocks.

This is why those funds which focus on capital appreciation are deemed to be more appropriate for those investors who have a higher tolerance for risk. Growth funds are usually called capital appreciation investments since they pour their funds into company stocks which are rapidly expanding and boosting their shareholder values at the same time. They do employ capital appreciation as their primary investment strategy to meet the expectations of lifestyle and retirement investors.

Charles Schwab

The Charles Schwab Brokerage was created when "Chuck" Schwab started a discount brokerage in 1975. From this point on the company led the investing industry by innovating in a variety of ways. In 1982, they expanded their offerings to include 24 hours per day, 7 days per week service. They launched their financial advisor service in 1987. The company began providing low cost online trading to customers in 1996.

Charles Schwab began rating investments according to a quantitative fact basis in 2002. As of 2006, they started offering affordable and professional investment advice. The company provided ETF investing with no commissions from 2009. By 2015 they had begun their automated and simple investing program. This Schwab Intelligent Portfolios does all the work of building, investing, monitoring, and re-balancing portfolios for their clients with no commissions or fees. It allows them to easily invest and monitor their positions without having to invest significant time in research, selection, and monitoring.

All of this pioneering over the years has helped Charles Schwab to become a powerful force in the brokerage world. They serve investors, employers, and financial advisors all at once. As of September 30, 2016, they hold an impressive $2.73 trillion of client assets. They number 1.6 million participants in their corporate retirement plans. Clients maintain 1.1 million banking accounts with them. Seven thousand different registered investment advisors are served by their products and services.

Even though Charles Schwab has excelled as a telephone and internet based advisory service, they also maintain an extensive network of branches and financial consultants. This includes over 330 branches and around 1,200 financial consultants who work for them. Their advisory solutions counts over $210.2 billion under management. The company takes great pride in having delivered more than 100,000 different financial plans as of September 30, 2016.

Charles Schwab has always been sought out by motivated investors who took pride in their personal engagement with their investments. Their clients are typically committed to investing and have an understanding sense of ownership. They wish to make and control their financial futures for themselves.

All of these characteristics and traits of the brokerage company have paid off handsomely in terms of not only size and assets, but also with numerous awards for 2016 and earlier years. JD Power and Associates' 2016 Full Service Investor Satisfaction Study ranked Schwab the Highest in Investor Satisfaction Among Full Service Brokerage Firms.

Fortune Magazine chose Charles Schwab as one of its Top 50 Most Admired Companies in the World. The magazine gave them its number one rankings for their Innovation and Social Responsibility in Key Attributes of Reputation categories. They received the number two ranking for the category of Securities and Asset Management.

Gallup has also recognized Schwab with its Great Workplace Award. For the fifth year in a row in 2016, they took one of the top 35 spots for companies acknowledged for possessing workforces which are most engaged in the world.

The company celebrated its 40th anniversary in 2015. In this time, they have successfully navigated and led with being a telephone centered discount full service brokerage, a branch network based one, and an Internet platform brokerage services provider. Despite being discount, they still rank at the top of their category for client satisfaction, most admired companies, and engaged employees.

Common Stock

Common stocks are shares in an underlying company that represent equity ownership in the corporation. They are also known as ordinary shares. These are securities in which individuals invest their capital. Common stock is the opposite of preferred stock.

While common stock and preferred stock both represent ownership in the company, there are many important differences between the two. Should a company go bankrupt, common stock holders are only given their money after preferred stock owners, bond owners, and creditors. Yet, common stock performs well, typically seeing greater levels of price appreciation than does preferred stock.

Common stock typically comes with voting rights, another feature that preferred stock does not have. These votes are used in electing the board of directors at the company's annual meeting, as well as in determining such things as company strategy, stock splits, policies, mergers and acquisitions, and the sale of the company. Preemptive rights in common stocks refer to owners with these rights being allowed to keep the same proportion of ownership in the company' stock, even if it issues additional stock.

Common stocks do not always pay dividends to share holders, as preferred stocks typically do. The dividends of common stocks are not pre-set or fixed. This means that the dividend returns are not completely predictable. Instead, they are based on a company's reinvestment policies, earnings results, and practices of the market in the valuing of the stock shares themselves.

Common shares have various other benefits. They are typically less expensive than are preferred stock shares. They are more heavily traded and readily available as well. The spreads between the buying and selling prices on them tend to be tighter as a result. Common stocks generally provide capital appreciation as the price of the shares rises over time, assuming that the company continues to do well and meet or exceed expectations. Dividends are often paid to common share holders when these things prove to be the case.

Common stocks can be purchased in any denominated amount. Round lots of common stocks are sold by even one hundred share amounts. This means that five hundred shares of common stock would be considered to be five lots of common stock.

Common stocks represent principally capital gains types of investments, as an investor is looking to buy them low and sell them at a higher price. This leads to a capital gain when the stock is sold at this greater level. The capital gain is the difference between the selling price and the purchasing price. Common stocks can also be cash flow types of investments when they pay a reliable stream of dividends every quarter. These income amounts are typically smaller than the one time amounts realized in capital gains, though they are obtained four times per year on a quarterly basis, or occasionally more often on a monthly basis.

Deferred Annuity

A Deferred Annuity refers to a specific kind of annuity contract. These types of annuities delay income payments (in the form of either a lump sum or installments) to the point where the investor chooses to obtain them. There are two principal stages in these kinds of annuities. These are the savings phase and the income phase. In the savings phase, individuals put money into the contract. The income phase is the one after the annuity becomes converted so that the payments are distributed as arranged. With deferred annuities there are several sub-types. These include fixed, variable, equity-indexed, and longevity.

A Fixed Deferred Annuity operates similarly to a CD Certificate of Deposit. The main difference lies in how the interest income must be claimed. With these annuities, it becomes long-term deferred until the owners take disbursements from the contract. These fixed contracts come with a guaranteed rate of interest that all funds earn. The insurance company stands behind the guarantee. These are attractive choices for those investors who are averse to risk and who do not require any interest income until after they turn 59 and ½ or older.

A variable Deferred Annuity is something like an assortment of mutual funds. With annuities, they refer to these as sub-accounts. Each owner has personal control over the investment risk he or she engages in through selecting particular sub-accounts which may cover both stocks and bonds. The returns on these investments will influence how well the annuity performs. For most investors, it benefits them more to purchase shares in several index mutual funds. This is because deferring taxes to retirement could mean that the owners will possibly pay higher taxes when they are retired than when they are working. The fees can also be as high as greater than three percent each year with many variable annuities.

Equity indexed annuities work much like the fixed annuities but also have variable annuity-like features. They possess two features. The first proves to be a guaranteed minimum return. The second is the ability to obtain a higher return than this by gaining from a formula which is based on one of the popular indices of the stock market like the S&P 500 or the Dow Jones Industrial Average. The downside to this type is that it typically comes with expensive surrender charges that can last over a ten to fifteen consecutive year long period.

Buying one of these last categories, the longevity annuity, is akin to obtaining insurance for a long life expectancy. It is helpful to consider a real life example to better understand how this works out in practice. An investor who is 60 might decide to pay in $150,000 to one of these longevity annuities. In exchange for this consideration, the insurance company which backs it will promise to pay out a set dollar amount of income for the rest of the holder's life beginning 25 years later at age 85. The advantage to this type of arrangement is that the retirees can then spend their other retirement assets because they feel comfortable that there will be a steady income stream that will support them guaranteed the rest of their lives. All income and taxes would be deferred to the distribution age when the money begins being disbursed.

It is important to realize with these annuities that any early withdrawals realized before the owners reach their legal retirement age will come with a full 10 percent penalty tax on top of the regular income taxes which the IRS will assess. The income tax rate would be based on the tax bracket of the individual when they receive the distribution.
These deferred annuities have many interesting (but often expensive) options and features which the buyers can obtain. Some of these include future income guarantees and death benefits.

Defined Benefit Plan

A defined benefit plan is a pension plan that serves as a vehicle for retirement. These plans give owners who are retiring benefits that are already pre-determined when they are established. These plans turn out to be a win-win situation for all parties.

Employees like the set benefit towards retirement that this provides. Employers also appreciate particular features of the plan. An employer is able to make larger contributions with this type of plan than with a defined contribution plan. Businesses can deduct the amounts they contribute from their tax liabilities. These types of plans are more complicated than the defined contribution plans. This is what sets the two types of plans apart. Defined benefit plans are more expensive to set up and to maintain than are alternative employee benefit plans.

What makes these plans more helpful to employees is the contributor. Employers usually contribute the most to them. Cases exist where employees can make voluntary contributions of their own. Occasionally the plan requires employees to make contributions. Whoever contributes, the benefits delivered by the plan are limited. The IRS sets and changes these limits every few years.

There are numerous distinctive features to these types of plans. An advantage to defined benefit plans is that plan participants can be allowed to take a loan against the value of the plan. Distributions before the participant reaches 62 are usually not allowed while the employee is still working for the company. The employees with the defined benefit plans are allowed to participate in other retirement plans.

Businesses have certain requirements with these plans as well. Companies of all sizes can participate in one. They are able to offer other types of retirement plans as well. Participating companies need to have an actuary who is enrolled in the plan decide how much the funding levels should be. Businesses also may not decrease the plan benefits after they have set them.

There are many advantages to defined benefit plans. Companies can confer significant retirement benefits on employees in a small amount of time. Employees can earn these benefits in a similarly short time frame. Even early retirement does not eliminate the ability to access these benefits. Employers appreciate that they can put more into these plans than with alternatives plans Employees love the predictable dollar benefits that the plans deliver. They also are happy to have a retirement account whose benefits do not depend on investment returns.

The schedule for becoming vested in the money of this benefit account varies. It can be set up for immediate full vesting. Schedules for vesting can stretch to as long as seven years with defined benefit plans as well. Some employers use the flexibility with these accounts to provide an early retirement package. Offering special benefit packages for early retirement is achievable with defined benefit plans.

There are also several downsides to these types of plans. They are the most complicated plan to administer and run. Defined benefit plans are also the most expensive kind of retirement benefit plan that a company can offer.

The IRS penalizes companies that do not make their minimum contribution requirement for a year. They do this using an excise tax when the minimums are not met. Some companies may wish to make larger contributions to the plan than they need to do. They might be motivated by the larger tax breaks. If a company over contributes, than an excise tax also applies.

Defined Contribution Plans

Defined contribution plans turn out to be a specific type of retirement plan. In these, an employer's yearly dollar amount contribution to the plan is spelled out clearly. Accounts are established on an individual basis for all employees participating. The amounts that are credited to such accounts include both the preset employer contributions, as well as any contributions coming from an employee. On top of this, earnings on investments are also accrued in defined contribution plan accounts.

With defined contribution plans, solely the contributions from employers are pledged to the accounts. Future benefits are not assured. In such plans, the benefits in the future go up and down based on the results of earnings on investments held in the plans.

Savings and thrift plans prove to be the most generally seen type of defined contribution plans. With this kind of a plan, employees put in to the account a pre arranged percentage of their typically pre taxed earnings. The monies go to the employee's individual account. Part of the contributions, or all of them in some cases, are then matched up by the employee's employer.

Once these pre set contributions are credited to the individual employees' accounts from both employees and employers, these contributions are subsequently invested. They might be invested in to the stock market, for example. The resulting investment returns are finally appointed to the account on an individual basis. This is the case whether the returns prove to be positive or negative.

When retirement time arrives for an employee, the participant's account then pays out benefits for retirement. This can occur through the account buying an annuity that will then assure a regular stream of income. In recent years, these defined contribution plans have expanded to be found in nearly all countries. For numerous nations, these are currently the main type of plan for the private sector retirement schemes. This growth in defined contribution plans has occurred at the expense of defined benefit plans, also known as pension plans, as employers seek to avoid the considerable expenses in funding and maintaining pension plans.

Money that is put into these defined contribution plans may come from employer contributions or salary deferral of an employee. These plans over time have evolved to become fairly easily portable from one job and company to the next as an employee changes companies. This did not always turn out to be the case.

One unique feature of defined contribution plans revolve around the rewards and risks of investments undertaken. Every employee is responsible for his or her own account's performance, rather than the employer or sponsor of the plan. Besides this, employees are not made to buy annuities with the retirement savings. This means that they could theoretically live beyond their retirement assets, and they take on the risk of this possibility. In Great Britain, the law requires that the majority of the retirement funds be employed in buying an annuity so that this does not happen.

Economic Participation

Economic Participation refers to the labor rate of participation. This means that it measures the total active population participating in the labor force. Another way of saying this is that it pertains to the numbers of individuals which are actively seeking out work or who are already employed. The two categories are important to consider, as in economic recessions a number of active labor force workers will despair of finding a job and simply give up the search for employment. This means that the Economic Participation rate will decrease as this happens.

Such an Economic Participation rate is a key measurement to utilize when considering a body of unemployment statistics. This is because it reveals the numbers of those individuals who show interest in being a part of the active work force. Such people either have a job or are actively looking for one. They usually must be considered from 16 to 18 years of age or older to be eligible for inclusion in the category. Those individuals who are not physically capable of working or who lack the interest in working will not comprise the participation rate. This includes retirees, imprisoned people, students, and homemakers or stay at home moms.

This is an important metric to consider alongside the official unemployment rates. The reason is that many individuals who are called unemployed might not really be true participants in the active work force. If analysts only contemplate the unemployment rate by itself, they might arrive at the conclusion that a greater number of individuals are not bringing home income.

This does not meant that they are not actively contributing to the level of the economy. It might be that such individuals choose not to work for a variety of reasons. They could be spending retirement savings, building their skills as college or university students, or spending their spouse's earnings as stay at home moms. It explains why both unemployment statistics and the Economic Participation rate should be reviewed together to fully appreciate the true employment picture of an economy and country.

This Economic Participation rate becomes even more critical to understand when recessions bite. As an economy goes from reasonably good to particularly bad, many workers will simply give up looking for work after many months unemployed. At this point, they could simply abandon the workforce. The labor participation rate would then decline. The reason is that these individuals would no longer be classified as actively looking for employment. This explains why in recessions, sudden plunges in the labor participation rate would be carefully considered and evaluated.

A case in point is the effects of the Great Recession on the ongoing Economic Participation rate. The labor force impact from this worst economic collapse since the Great Depression of the 1930's proved to be absolutely devastating. The recession officially began in December of 2007. Per the NBER National Bureau of Economic Research, the unemployment rate stood at 5 percent that month. When the recession officially ended in June of 2009, this unemployment rate reached 9.5 percent and then climbed on to peak out at 10 percent by October of 2009.

In the eight years since then, the unemployment rate has nearly touched five percent again. Yet the labor participation rate has never recovered from the Great Recession. Many economists believe that this devastating recession and global financial collapse caused the acceleration of structural changes in the labor force participation rate. The rate has ranged from 67 percent back in 2006 to today's near 62 percent in 2017.

The decrease in the economic participation rate has been broad based and consistent since 2009 in fact. Many baby boomers decided to retire early as their job opportunities suddenly evaporated. Many individuals used government grants and loans to go back to university or college. Some women stopped working to be stay at home moms as the job opportunities were so scarce.

Employee Stock Ownership Plan (ESOP)

An Employee Stock Ownership Plan refers to a type of retirement plan. They are also called by their acronym ESOP. These plans permit employing companies to either provide cash or stock shares directly to the employee benefits plan. These plans hold one account for every employee who participates in them. The stock shares that the employers contribute become vested over a pre-determined period of years.

Once they are partially or fully vested, employees are able to access them. It is important to note that with these ESOPs, employees never actually hold or purchase the shares of the stock directly when they are employees of the firm. Once the employee becomes retired, fired, disabled, or deceased, the stock shares become distributed.

One should never confuse an Employee Ownership Stock Plan with an employee stock option plan. These stock option plans are not really retirement plans. Rather they only provide the right to purchase the company stock for a given, pre-determined price in a certain time period.

One benefit that makes these Employee Stock Ownership Plans popular with providers and participants alike is their tax advantaged status. The reason they are considered to be qualified is because the company participating, the shareholder who sells, and the participants are each able to enjoy varying tax benefits. This is why these ESOPs are typically utilized by companies as part of their corporate financial strategy at the same time they are employed to encourage the employees to be sympathetic to the company stakeholders and their interests.

Without a doubt, the Employee Stock Ownership Plan is part and parcel of the compensation that employees enjoy from their company. This is why they are utilized to keep the employees working for the overall good of the company as a whole. They have a stake in the stock share price rising over time since they are part owners in the company stock.

These benefits from the Employee Stock Ownership Plan accrue to the employees at no upfront cost. The shares are kept for the receiving employees in a trust to ensure they grow safely to the point where the employee resigns or retires (or is fired).

These companies are actually employee-owned to some degree. Employee-owned corporations are those that have a majority of their shares in the hands of the company employees. This makes them cooperatives but for the fact that the firm's capital is unevenly distributed. Much of the time, such employee-owned corporations do not provide voting rights to all of the shareholders. Besides this, the senior-most employees and management will always have the distinct advantage of receiving a greater number of shares than the newer employees.

There are several other competing forms of employee ownership benefits. Among these are stock options, direct purchase plans, phantom stock, restricted stock, and stock appreciation rights. Stock options give their employees the chance to purchase shares of company stock for a set price in a fixed amount of time. A direct purchase plan permits employees to buy their shares in the company using their own after tax dollars.

Phantom stock delivers special cash bonuses in reward for superior employee results. The bonus amounts equal to the sale price of a certain quantity of stock shares. Restricted stock provides employees the ability to obtain shares either in the form of gift or by buying them, once they have met certain minimum employment period benchmarks. Stock appreciation rights provide employees with the ability to increase the value of a pre-assigned quantity of shares. Such shares typically become actually payable in the form of cash.

ERISA

ERISA is the acronym for The Employment Retirement Income Security Act that was enacted in 1974. This ERISA legislation set up a basic level of standards for health, retirement, and various additional types of plans for welfare benefits. These include disability insurance, life insurance, and apprenticeship plans.

This Employment Retirement Income Security Act is both overseen and run by the EBSA, which turns out to be the acronym for Employee Benefits Security Administration. This EBSA operates as a division under the United States DOL, or Department of Labor. If you have any questions about the act, concerns that you are not being treated according to the law, or complaints regarding treatment as the ERISA laws relate to you, then you should contact your area ERISA office for help and clarification.

It is important to note that these protecting regulations mandated by ERISA only pertain to non government, private employers who choose to provide benefits plans and health insurance that is employer sponsored for their employees. ERISA does not force such employers to provide such these plans for employees. Rather, it only lays out regulations for the employee offered benefits that such employers make available. It is also significant that the rules and regulations set up by ERISA do not pertain to those benefits or insurance policies that are purchased by an individual privately.

ERISA does establish the requirements and standards for a number of different related elements. Reporting and accountability is required to be detailed and made available to the U.S. Federal government. The conduct for HMO's and other managed care, as well as for other people who have financial responsibility for the administration of the plan, is strictly regulated by the ERISA rules.

ERISA also pertains to safeguards and procedures. Written policies have to be set up to determine the way that claims have to be filed, along with the claims' appeals process in writing for any claims that are denied. ERISA further stipulates that these appeals should be decided in a reasonably timed and fair way. ERISA also proves to be a protection that insures that all plans are both offered, safeguarded, and funded in the ways that most appropriately favor the members and their best interests.

ERISA does not permit discrimination in the ways that benefits in the plan are gathered and collected for those members who are qualified. Finally, ERISA insists that a variety of disclosures be made to the participants in the plan. These include a plan summary that specifically lists out the provided benefits, the associated rules for obtaining such benefits, any limitations of the plans, and other matters including getting referrals before doctor and surgeon visits.

ESOP

An ESOP stands for the Employee Stock Ownership Plan. These are not exactly retirement savings accounts in the traditional sense. They are critical investment vehicles with tax advantages. With these types of accounts, employers establish a trust fund for the employee. The employer is then able to transfer shares of its own stock to this fund.

They might alternatively allocate cash with which the employees' account can purchase already existing shares of stock. These ESOPs prove to be the most typical means for employees gaining part ownership in their company within the United States.

Every company has its own unique formulas for allocating shares to its participating employees. The shares come out of the company trust account and transfer over to the appropriate individual employee accounts. As with other benefits for employees that are employer sponsored, vesting rules apply.

Gaining full vesting in stock option accounts requires the employee to reach a minimum number of years at the company. Once this seniority level and vesting is obtained, the employee fully owns the shares and may sell them at will. When employees part with the company, the vested shares of stock have to be purchased from them at the full market price.

There are also tax benefits to these stock option plans. Companies that issue them accrue the advantages of tax deductions for the stock value. Employees do not have to pay any taxes on employer offered contributions. They are also able to transfer the distributions to IRAs or other qualified retirement vehicles. This will help them to avoid realizing capital gains or income taxes.

These stock option plans do have limitations and rules pertaining to rollovers and withdrawals. Distribution rules can be different from one employer to the next. In general the distributions are allowed to be rolled over to other retirement plans which are qualified. Any person with an ESOP will find the distribution rules detailed in the Summary Plan Description section.

As with 401(k)s and other types of retirement vehicles, penalties for early withdrawals do apply. An employee must be 59 ½ to begin receiving non penalized distributions. These distributions become mandatory on the April 1st that follows the year the employee reaches 70 ½. Companies have the choices of making these account distributions with cash, stocks, or a combination of the two.

Regardless of the way they give them out, employees are always allowed to sell back vested stock shares. The proceeds from these sold shares can be transferred into self directed or traditional IRAs to defer taxes. They may also roll or transfer their distributions to a different company's qualified retirement savings vehicle. The money will only become taxable at ordinary income tax rates once it is withdrawn later.

Participants in these stock option plans are not able to purchase any types of gold investments with the distributions. The only exceptions are when an employee has obtained diversification rights from his or her employer. Normally only employees of gold mining companies would be able to acquire either paper or physical gold in such a retirement savings account.

Because of these limitations, rolling over distributions from a stock option account to a self directed IRA makes sense. Once the funds are in a self directed account, the holders will be able to choose where they invest these funds. They will then have a variety of tax free alternative investments such as gold and other precious metals.

There are a few downsides to the employer established and funded profits sharing plans. Investment choices are as limited as can be imagined. The account owner also has to complete the company's vesting schedule. This means that the employees can only access their funds once the vesting period of years has elapsed. ESOP's also carry risks specific to the employee's company. Should the employer go bankrupt, the plan may become closed. An employee might no longer be allowed to contribute to the plan or account at this point.

Expense Ratio

Expense ratio relates to the costs that a mutual fund incurs as it trades and does normal business. Typical mutual fund expense ratios include a number of different costs. Among these are management fees, transaction costs, custody costs, marketing fees, legal expenses, and transfer agent fees.

Management fees comprise those charges that the fund pays to the company which handles the portfolio management. They invest the fund's money as per the direction of the mutual fund board of directors. Management costs are typically the largest single portion of the mutual fund's expenses.

These fees commonly range from as little as .5% to as much as 2%. Lower fees are usually more advantageous for investors. This is because every dollar that goes to the management of the fund is not increasing the share holders' wealth. Some mutual fund types charge a higher amount in fees. International or global mutual funds will usually cost more than simple domestic market mutual funds. They justify these greater charges by the difficulty of managing an international portfolio.

Transaction costs include the fees that the fund pays to stock brokers. These are negotiated to extremely low rates such as a penny per share or even lower thanks to the enormous volumes that mutual funds trade. Those funds that are constantly purchasing and selling investments create significantly greater transacting costs for themselves and their investors. Higher turnover rates like this also can lead to larger capital gains taxes and other costs.

The investment holdings of a mutual fund must be kept by a custodian bank. This creates custody costs where these banks register the bonds, stocks, and other investments for the fund. Some of the banks do this electronically and others keep actual stock certificates in their vault storage.

Custodian banks also collect interest and dividend payments, maintain accounting for the various positions so gain/loss info is readily available to management, and handle stock splits and other transaction issues. These

custodian costs prove to be a less significant percentage of exper for the mutual funds.

Marketing fees for mutual funds come out of the money that the inve pool. This money is utilized to advertise the fund so they can raise additional investment dollars. More money in the fund means more management fees for the portfolio managers. These 12b-1 marketing are money that does not benefit an investor after the fund exceeds $1(million in net assets. A very small number of brokers actually refund su fees to their investors.

There are some legal expenses that mutual funds must incur in the cours of normal operating business. These include for paperwork they are required by law to file for regulators like the SEC, specific licenses, incorporation, and other legal procedures. The majority of funds count such costs as a small amount of their overall expense ratio.

Transfer agent costs cover the expenses that arise when a shareholder cashes out or buys into the fund. Transfer agents must handle various account statements, paperwork, and money in the process. These agents take care of all the mundane daily paperwork for purchases, redemptions, and processing which keep the fund and other capital markets working.

There are various other costs that are not included in the mutual fund expense ratio but many experts feel should be. These include mutual fund sales loads. These fees are simply commissions that go into the pocket of the institution, company, or stockbroker that persuaded you to buy the mutual fund in the first place. Because of these and other high costs of many mutual fund expense ratios, some people prefer low cost index funds that involve very low management costs.

Face Value

Face Value represents the dollar value of a given security as the issuer states it officially. It is also otherwise known as the nominal value. Where stocks are concerned, this is the certificate-displayed original value of the stock. With bonds, this amounts to the dollar amount which will be paid back to the bond holder when the bond matures. This amount for bonds is usually $1,000 par value. Where bonds are concerned, this value is also called par value or sometimes only "par." Par value is very important with bonds, while it means little to stock investors.

Par value is two completely different concepts when dealing with bonds versus stocks. With bonds, this refers to the full amount which the company will return to the bondholder at the time of maturity. This assumes that the issuer does not default on its bond principal. Despite this set face value to be returned at maturity, bonds which trade on the secondary market have market values which fluctuate every trading day based largely on the prevailing interest rates.

As an example, when interest rates prove to be greater than the coupon rate on the bond, the issue will be sold on the secondary market at a discount to par value. This means that the price will be lower than the par. At the same time, when interest rates turn out to be lower than the coupon rate of the bond, the bond sells for a premium, at higher than par. The par value still guarantees a fixed principal return in any case. Yet this value is considered to be a bad indicator of the current worth for the bond, given the fact that very few bonds actually trade for par on the secondary market.

Bond holders can make additional profits over their fixed interest rate. This opportunity lies in buying the bond at below face value, then holding it to receive the par at maturity date. This gap between sub-par purchase price on the secondary market and the par value at maturity becomes pure profit to the bond holder if they hold the bond until that eventual date is reached.

The face value where stocks are concerned is quite different from that par with bonds. The importance of stock shares' par value as stated on their shares pertains to the legal amount of capital which the business must maintain. It is a fact that only cash the company has in excess of this total

amount (number of shares times the share par value) may be paid out in the form of dividends to the investors. In practice this means that the face value of the shares serves as a type of corporate cash reserve.

The law does not mandate how much the stated par value has to be when it is issued. Businesses could sidestep the reserve requirement effect by applying laughably low values to the share certificates. Examples of two prominent companies illustrate this strategy well. AT&T shares have only $1 per common share listed as their par value. Stock giant Apple shares trading at hundreds of dollars apiece list a par value of merely $0.00001 per share, a ridiculous face value amount in practice.

This is why a stock or even bond's face value rarely if ever determines the true market value of the relevant issue, especially with stocks. The market value is only based upon the market forces of supply and demand. This is decided in practice by how much investors will willingly pay for buying and selling shares on a given security at a particular snap shot moment in time. If market conditions are right, the par value and actual market value at any given moment may have little or nothing to do with each other.

With bonds and their markets, it is all about the prevailing interest rates and how they correlate to the coupon rate of the bond. This will generally decide whether the bond sells at, above, or below its par value. With zero coupon bonds, investors do not receive any interest besides buying the bond for less than its face value. These are sold for less than par as the sole means for investors to realize any profits in this case.

Fixed Annuity

A Fixed Annuity refers to a particular form of annuity contract. Insurance companies make such contracts with individuals who are mostly saving for retirement or estate planning. Two main types of these annuities exist, variable and fixed annuities. The fixed one permits investors to add money to the account which is tax deferred. The investor furnishes a lump sum of money in exchange for which the life insurance provides a fully guaranteed and fixed interest rate at the same time as they also guarantee 100 percent of the principle invested. These annuities are often popular for their ability to offer the annuity holder (annuitant) a fully guaranteed income on a regular basis. This can be arranged as a specific number of years or for the remainder of the individual's life.

The motivation for a person to turn over a large sum of money to an insurance company for such a Fixed Annuity lies in the wish to obtain guaranteed returns while not having any original principal at risk. The second factor centers on the special tax advantages that these contracts with insurance companies enjoy. They receive many of the identical tax advantages from which life insurance policies benefit. Among these are earnings growth on a tax-deferred basis. This does not mean that taxes will not be paid, only that they will not be due until the contract becomes annuitized into monthly payouts or the earnings in the account become withdrawn.

There are a number of advantages to these types of Fixed Annuity investments that continue to draw investors to them year in and out. They offer guaranteed minimum rates, competitive yields which are fixed, guaranteed income payments, withdrawal ability, tax deferred growth, and principal safety.

The guaranteed minimum rates are nice but not forever it is important to note. These exist for an initial period only. The subsequent rates becomes adjusted utilizing a certain formula or alternatively employing whatever the prevailing yield is in the investment accounts of the insurers. Some fixed annuities will also offer an extended minimum rate guarantee as a protection in case interest rates decline in the future.

Competitive yields that are fixed come from the life insurance firm's investment portfolio which generates them. These investments mostly go into both high quality corporate bonds and U.S. government bonds. This yield is usually greater than a comparable yield on another investment which comes without risk. Many times this will be guaranteed by the insurance company for anywhere from at least one to as many as ten years.

To many annuity buyers, the guaranteed income payments are the greatest benefit to them. This feature becomes activated when the holder converts the fixed annuity into what is known as an immediate annuity. They can do this whenever they wish to provide a fully guaranteed monthly income payout that can last the remainder of the annuitant's life if they so desire.

Withdrawals are possible with these forms of Fixed Annuities. Holders can take an annual withdrawal every year that is as high as 10 percent of the value of the account. Any amounts greater than 10 percent will be penalized with a surrender charge if this occurs during the surrender period (usually ranging from seven to 12 years from contract start). Every year this surrender charge amount decreases until it eventually reaches zero. At that point withdrawals exceeding 10 percent of the account become penalty-free. There would still be the IRS tax penalty which amounts to ten percent (plus regular income taxes levied as well) on any withdrawals made before the owner reaches 59 and ½ years of age.

Principal safety is a rare commodity in these financially unstable times in the world. Annuities guarantee this, but the strength of the guarantee is only as good as the life insurance company that makes it. This is why investors should only invest their money with those life insurance firms which have at least an A or higher financial strength rating.

Fixed Income

Fixed Income refers to the kind of budgeting and investing style that delivers periodic income and actual returns back to the owners of the investments. This income goes out in generally predictable amounts in frequent and anticipated intervals. The investors who flock to fixed income investments are usually retirees. They count on such periodic returns from investments to give them a stable and regular stream of income. Thanks to the dependable returns they provide, this type of investment is heavily preferred by the demographic of older investors.

Fixed income also defines a style of investing whose goal is to provide a general stream of stable and fixed income. Where individual lifestyles are concerned, it also relates to the income of a specific household or a particular individual. Mutual funds can be of this type of investing strategy. This portion of the funds will be invested in vehicles that provide low risk and which pay out interest or dividends. Bonds or mutual funds containing bonds are classic examples of these kinds of investments.

It is true that fixed income is most popular with retirees for a good reason. At this point in these investors' lives, they need to count on both predictable and stable returns and regular income. It is the income sources such as investment returns, pensions, Social Security payouts, annuities, and other funds that generate the more or less same level of income retired individuals find necessary to sustain a given lifestyle from year to year. This is the reason that retirees are also a good explanation of the phrase fixed income. Their income is fixed, so they can not absorb additional costs and increases in living expenses.

Because the point of overall fixed income investment strategy is for guaranteeing a dependable stream of income, these investment fund advisors generally favor dividend yielding mutual funds, bonds, certificates of deposit, differing kinds of annuities, and money market funds.

Bonds still remain among the most common and popular of these fixed income investments today. Large corporations, local governments like municipalities and counties, state and provincial governments, and national governments all issue such bonds of different types. These investments provide a nice income for not only retirees but also other investors who are on the lookout for a diversified portfolio. The percentages of a portfolio dedicated to fixed income will vary depending on the individual investor's needs and preference (or tolerance) for risk.

As an example, an investor could allocate a portfolio to the following fixed income categories. They might choose 50 percent to investment grade bonds, 20 percent to high yield bonds, 15 percent to Treasuries, and 15 percent to international bonds. Those products which are considered to be riskier, like longer maturity instruments and junk rated bonds, should always be a small percentage of the total portfolio in question. Naturally bonds which are riskier will pay a higher amount of interest or coupon rate since there is a greater chance of risk.

Besides bond yields, investors who are seeking income that is fixed have other choices for returns. There are interest paying investments like CDs and money market funds available.

Examples of concerns that affect fixed income instruments are important to consider. Borrowers can default on bonds, even those these are generally considered to be safe investments (though junk bonds are usually not). There are also exchange rate risks involved with international bonds. Longer maturity date fixed investments are also subject to a risk of interest rates going up over time, which could reduce the asset value of the underlying instrument. This is because where bonds are concerned interest rates and values are inversely correlated.

Fund Manager

Fund managers are the individuals, investment companies, or sometimes banks that handle a mutual fund's investment decisions. These decision makers are charged with earning as much profit for their fund as they reasonably can while still following the risk parameters that the mutual fund discloses.

Fund managers are compensated differently than stock brokers who earn commissions. These managers receive their compensation based on the total dollar amounts under the management of the mutual fund. An advantage to this form of payment is that it provides motivation for fund managers to increase overall assets. A more successful manager will attract more investors and money and achieve greater returns. The management fee that the fund levies pays the fund manager. This fee appears on fund financials under the expense ratio.

A mutual fund's board of directors hires the fund manager. Fund shareholders themselves select the board of directors. These fund managers wear many hats. They oversee all of the investments that the mutual fund undertakes. They must set and manage annual meetings. They must also be responsible for the mutual fund's customer service efforts and many different elements of fund compliance. Compliance roles include offering a fund prospectus, negotiating commission rates with brokers, issuing proxies, and other important periodic and daily tasks.

Fund managers generally hire staff to help them with these many roles. Sometimes they contract out some or all of these services to another company. In practice most mutual funds are owned by families of mutual fund companies. In these cases, these companies provide their fund managers with these services at a cost.

A number of mutual funds have single managers in charge of the fund. The majority of larger funds have significant sized staffs that the fund manager leads. In such cases, these leadership positions are more like investment managers than fund managers. The biggest funds have a few fund managers who share the responsibilities and decisions. Entire investment firms act as fund managers to some mutual funds.

A fund manager is an important person to consider when investors are looking at mutual funds. One of the most important characteristics of a successful mutual fund concerns how long the fund manager has been present. Funds which boast a fund manager who has been with them a long time have a distinct advantage.

If a fund claims significant changes in its fund management, this is generally looked at as a negative factor. It might indicate that there have been problems in the fund with the performance. It could also imply that the fund manager has not properly carried out compliance and other critical issues in the daily running of the fund. Alternatively, a change in fund manager could simply mean that the fund has overhauled its investment strategy and changed its emphasis.

Hedge funds also employ fund managers. A hedge fund manager is far less restricted in the investments that he or she can pursue than is a mutual fund manager. This is because there is much less regulation for hedge funds than for mutual funds.

The hedge fund managers receive their income according to a different compensation scheme. Mutual fund managers earn their fees however the fund performs. Hedge fund managers instead are rewarded with a percentage of their earned returns. They also receive a small management fee that commonly runs between one and four percent of the fund's net asset value.

Investors who do not like paying managers for poor performance appreciate this structure for paying hedge fund managers. The disadvantage to it concerns risk. Hedge fund managers could pursue more aggressive and risky strategies to make greater returns because of their fee structure.

Gold Roth IRA

Gold Roth IRA's are IRA's that are allowed to contain gold and other precious metals. Gold Roth IRA's make sense for many investors. This is because gold and other precious metals like silver and platinum have been considered to be the greatest form of long term storage for cash and valuables throughout history.

This means that gold in particular could be considered to be the best asset for retirement. Although there are many other types of instruments used for retirement accounts and planning, including bonds, stocks, savings, and annuities, gold is the only one whose final value does not rest on an institution or individual's performance or success. This makes physical gold an ideal means for saving for retirement.

Gold Roth IRA's are specially created either through initially funding one or by rolling over a Roth IRA or traditional IRA to a gold backed Roth IRA. Rolling over an existing employee held 401K to a Gold Roth IRA can be difficult if the employee has not left the company. This is because employees are not usually allowed to do rollovers until they separate from their company.

IRA's that already exist can be transferred to Gold Roth IRA's. They can be moved from credit unions, banks, or stock broker firms to a trust company that is allowed to hold your Gold IRA holdings. In this type of transfer, you could choose to move securities held in the account along with cash, or cash by itself.

Gold Roth IRA's must be created by sending in cash to the administrator of the IRA. They will then purchase the gold, silver, or platinum physical holdings as you instruct them. The gold must then be kept by a gold IRA custodian on your behalf. These depositories provide safe places for the gold, as well as easy access to buy or sell it. The gold kept in a Gold Roth IRA may not be sent to your house or assumed in your personal possession. Instead, it has to be liquidated before the funds from it can be accessed. Gold that is requested as a distribution will be penalized at your personal tax rate plus a ten percent penalty.

Only certain forms of gold and precious metals are allowed to be purchased and held within a Gold Roth IRA. Gold bars have to demonstrate a twenty-four karat purity to be eligible. They can be one ounce, ten ounces, a kilogram, one hundred ounces, or four hundred ounces in size. Gold coins that are permitted are twenty-four karat bullion coins from the United States, Canada, Austria, and Australia. The most heavily minted gold coins of all time, the South Africa Krugerrand's, are not permitted, as they are only twenty-two karats.

Silver bars and coins that have .999 or higher purity are permitted to be held in a Gold Roth IRA account. This allows the Canadian Silver Maple Leaf, the U.S. Silver Eagle, and the Mexican Silver Libertad one ounce bullion coins. Silver bars that are one hundred ounces and one thousand ounces are also permitted.

Government Debt

Government debt refers to the total amount of government issued IOUs which have not been paid back at any given point. Governments issue such debt any time they chose to borrow money from the public or from overseas nations and companies.

As a government borrows this money, it provides government securities that give all of the important information on this investment debt. The face of the certificates states the interest rate which the government will pay on the original principal, the amount which they are borrowing, and the payment schedule for both principal pay back and interest payments. These outstanding securities are equal to the total debt amount which the government has not paid back. It is also the government debt.

Governments actually issue a variety of debt types. Economists classify such debt in different categories. The first would be by the form of governmental agency that issued such debt in the first place. Within the U.S., the principal governmental agencies which issue debt are state, federal, and local jurisdictions. Local debt is also further subdivided into sub-classes including city-, county-, or parish-issued government debt. All of these are considered a type of government bonds.

Yet another way to classify such government debt is according to the dates of maturity. This is why bond investors and U.S. Treasury officials with the Federal Reserve discuss thirty year and ten year bonds. These are the amounts of time between when the government originally issued the bond and the due date of the principal. With federal government debt, there are three easy to understand and remember types of maturities.

Treasury Bills are the first of these. They come with maturities amounting to a single year or under. This could be three month T-bills or year long T-bills. Treasury notes are the second designation. They have maturities that range from a single year to ten years long. Treasury bonds are the over ten year long maturity dates. With local or state level government debt, the terminology used is just bonds. This is true regardless of when they mature.

There are also bonds that carry infinite repayments. Analysts call these perpetuity bonds. With these bonds, the principal never becomes repaid. Interest payments will then be made forever. This would practically be until the government defaults, the country collapses financially, or the government buys back the bonds. Such bonds were at one time issued by the government of Great Britain. They called these consols.

A final means for classifying government debt bonds comes down to the revenue source which underlies the bonds' repayment. Those government debts that the entity plans to repay by utilizing revenues they garner from taxing their constituents they call general obligation bonds. Revenue bonds are those bonds that they pay back by employing particular user fees, sometimes from the project itself which the bonds will finance. This could be tolls on a new highway or a bridge. Only local and state government debt is classified this way.

The United States government debt has radically and exponentially increased over the past 15 to 20 years. Consider that in 2004 early in the year, the outstanding federal government debt amounted to around $7.1 trillion. In early 2017, that amount topped $20 trillion for the first time ever. Roughly half of this enormous debt amount the government owes to its pension funds - the Social Security Trust and Medicare Trust Funds.

Some economists like to say that the internal debt does not carry any public welfare or economic impacts, but they are incorrect with this assertion. Since the Social Security Fund will start to need its loaned out money paid back in 2020, it will require the government to issue either new debt to non-governmental buyers or to raise taxes dramatically to pay back the pension funds for the social security recipients' monthly benefits to continue.

This problem will only worsen over time through 2032 or 2033, when the funds will have exhausted all of their money the government owes them back. At this point, the federal government will either have to abandon the Social Security and Medicare programs entirely, dramatically reduce the benefits to where they are sustainable, hugely increase the age when retirees can draw on them, or vastly increase government revenues from somewhere.

Household Income

Household Income refers to the total income earned by all family members living in a single house. They must be fifteen years or older for their income to count. An interesting point is that the individuals living together do not have to be related at all to be considered a part of the overall household. This is a crucial measurement of risk that many lenders employ for underwriting loans. It also proves to be a helpful economic metric for grasping the standard of living in a given area.

The statistic of median household incomes is a commonly cited and released economic statistic within the United States. It can be misleading though, since a great number of American households are actually made up of only one person. This is why the statistic consistently plays second fiddle to median family income, which is similarly often reported as a leading economic indicator. Households which only consist of one person are not factored in to the average family income formula. This is why considering household income statistics can be constructive when analysts are attempting to do comparative measurements of living standards and true wealth from one state, city, county, or even country and the next.

Yet this household income remains among the three most frequently cited metrics for individual wealth in America today. The remaining two are per capita income and family income. These use a bit different means of approaching the standard of living for people in a certain jurisdiction and determining their overall financial wellbeing.

In fact, household income takes into account all incomes of any individual within the home who is at least fifteen years old. The weakness of the measurement lies in the fact that it similarly considers a single person dwelling alone to be an entire household as much as it would a family of seven. With the competing metric of family income, only those households which at least two people who are related via marriage, birth, or adoption are considered to be a true household.

Contrast this with per capita income, the third related measurement of individual and household wealth and standards of living. With per capita income, the measurement is the most true and accurate, since it considers only every individual person who dwells in a prescribed region, city, nation, or other area along and as themself. This means that two individual income earners within the same household or even family will always be counted distinctively under the formula for deriving per capita income.

Modern-day economists and analysts like to deploy household income all the same. They prefer it for drawing up a raft of conclusions regarding the overall economic health of a certain population group or regional area. As an example, economists will frequently compare the median household incomes from one nation of the world to many others.

This delivers a big picture as to what quality of life the citizens of various countries enjoy as compared to their compatriots living in other nations. It helps them to determine which country's citizens boast the best quality of life. In 2013, Luxembourg enjoyed the highest median household income in the globe at a staggering $52,493. Surprisingly, the United States came in at only sixth with $43,585.

Another practical application of the household income figure pertains to the regional prices for real estate. This can tell analysts much about whether or not the housing market could be overheating. Experts in household finance continuously maintain their claim that homebuyers can only afford to pay as much as three times their yearly incomes on a home.

This means that the ratio of median household income as measured against median home sales pricing will tell the tale on if a given home price is too expensive for the typical area household's income. In the housing bubble of the first half of the 2000s decade, the median home prices across many regions of the nation, including Southern California and Miami in South Florida especially, proved to be as much as five times higher than the local area median household income, making them unaffordable for the average household to all intents and purposes.

Index Funds

Index funds are typically exchange traded funds or mutual funds. Their goal is to reproduce the actual movements of an underlying index for a particular financial market. They do this no matter what is happening in the overall stock markets.

There are several means of tracking such an index. One way of doing this is by purchasing and holding all of the index securities to the same proportion as they are represented in the index. Another way of accomplishing this is by doing a statistical sample of the market and then acquiring securities that are representative of it. A great number of the index funds are based on a computer model that accepts little to no input from people in its decision making of the securities bought and sold. This qualifies as a type of passive management when the index fund is run this way.

These index funds do not have active management. This allows them to benefit from possessing lesser fees and taxes in their accounts that are taxable. The low fees that are charged do come off of the investment returns that are otherwise mostly matching those of the index. Besides this, exactly matching an index is not possible since the sampling and mirroring models of this index will never be one hundred percent right. Such variances between an index performance and that of the fund are referred to as the tracking error, or more conversationally as a jitter.

A wide variety of index funds exist for you to choose from these days. They are offered by a number of different investment managers as well. Among the more typically seen indices are the FTSE 100, the S&P 500, and the Nikkei 225. Other indexes have been created that are so called research indexes for creating asset pricing models. Kenneth French and Eugene Fama created one known as the Three Factor Model. This Fama-French three factor model is actually utilized by Dimensional Fund Advisers to come up with their various index funds. Other, newer indexes have been created that are known as fundamentally based indexes. These find their basis in factors like earnings, dividends, sales, and book values of companies.

The underlying concept for developing index funds comes from the EMH, or efficient market hypothesis. This hypothesis claims that because stock analysts and fund managers are always searching for stocks that will do better than the whole market, this efficient competition among them translates to current information on a company's affairs being swiftly factored into the price of the stock. Because of this, it is generally accepted that knowing which stocks will do better than the over all market in advance is exceedingly hard. Developing a market index then makes sense as the inefficiencies and risks inherent in picking out individual stocks can be simply eliminated through purchasing the index fund itself.

Individual Retirement Account (IRA)

An IRA stands for Individual Retirement Account. IRA's offer two types of savings for retirement. They can either be tax free or tax deferred retirement plans. In the universe of IRA's, numerous different types of accounts exist. These are principally either traditional and standard IRA's or Roth IRA's as the most popular types. The various IRA's are helpful to different individuals based on the particular scenarios and end goals of every person.

Standard IRA's permit contributions of as much as $4,000 every year. These are contributions that are tax deductible, giving the IRA's their primary advantage as retirement accounts. People who are older than fifty are allowed to contribute more than the $4,000 maximum for the purposes of catching up for their approaching retirement. Any money put into the IRA is used to reduce your annual income amount, which lessens your overall tax liability for the year.

The tax is really only deferred though, since monies taken from an IRA will be taxed at the typical income tax rate for the individual when they are withdrawn, even if they are held in such an account until retirement. When the money is taken out earlier than this age of 59 ½, then an extra ten percent penalty is applied as well. There are exceptions to the penalty rule though. When these early withdrawn monies are utilized to buy a home or to pay for the tuition costs associated with higher education, then they are not penalized. The typical tax rate would still apply, although the penalty is waived in these two cases. This makes IRA's a good vehicle for investments that also give you the versatility of making significant purchases with the money.

Roth IRA's are the other principal type of IRA's. The government established these types of IRA account back in 1997 in an effort to assist those Americans in the middle class with their retirement needs. Roth IRA's do not turn out to be tax deductible. The upside is that they offer greater amounts of flexibility than do the typical IRA's. These contributions are allowed to be taken out whenever you want without a penalty or extra tax. Interest that the account earns is taxed if taken out before the first five years have passed. At the end of five years, the earnings and contributions both made are capable of being taken out without having to pay either taxes or penalties. The identical housing and education allowances that permit to standard IRA's pertain to Roth IRA's. The principal attraction of Roth IRA's is that they offer tax free income at retirement time.

It is worth noting that the Roth IRA's have their particular rules that keep them from being for everybody. If your income is higher than $95,000 in a year, then you will be barred from making the full contribution, and if it exceeds $110,000, then you will not be allowed to make a partial contribution. For married, filing jointly, the limits are $150,000 for full contributions and $160,000 for partial contributions.

Institutional Investor

Institutional investors turn out to be organizations or occasionally individuals which buy and sell securities in huge enough quantities and currency totals. They benefit from lower fees and commissions as well as special treatment from the market makers.

These large and powerful deep pocketed investors experience fewer regulations from the regulatory agencies as well since they naturally assume that they have a larger knowledge base and are sophisticated enough to protect themselves in their investing strategies. There are many different kinds of investors who qualify as institutional investors. Some of them are life insurance firms and pension funds.

These entities derive their money from a variety of sources, but in all cases they pool the funds in order to buy and sell real estate, stock and bond securities, and other alternative types of investment classes such as loans, commodities, precious metals, and artwork.

There are many different kinds of institutional investors such as hedge funds, pension funds, insurance companies, sovereign wealth funds, commercial banks, investment advisors, Real Estate Investment Trusts, mutual funds, and university endowments. Other operating firms that choose to invest their extra capital in such asset classes are also covered by the term. Some institutional investors are activist. This means that they may interfere with the internal workings and governance of the firm by using their substantial voting rights in the companies in which they own larger stakes to influence corporate decisions, investments, and behavior.

Institutional investors act as intermediaries between smaller retail investors and corporations. They are also significant sources of critical capital for the financial markets. Since they pool together their member investment dollars or Euros, these larger and more powerful investors effectively lessen the cost of capital to entrepreneurs at the same time as the efficiently diversify their clients' portfolios. Since they can impact the behavior of companies as well, this helps to reduce agency costs.

Institutional investors have several significant and game changing advantages over smaller, weaker retail investors. They possess enormous resources to invest as well as specialty knowledge that pertains to a variety of different investment options. Many of these choices are not even available to traditional retail investors at all. They also have longer term investing horizons as they are not limited to accumulation and distribution requirements of individual investors who will want to transition to retirement at some point.

Such institutions turn out to be the biggest movers and shakers within both supply and demand segments in the securities markets. This means that they transact the overwhelming majority of all trades on the major stock and bond market exchanges. Their choices and actions substantially impact the prices and bid/asks of most securities on the various markets.

This has led a number of retail investors to attempt to level the proverbial playing field of investing by researching the various filings of holdings the institutions make with the SEC Securities and Exchange Commission to learn what different securities they ought to invest in for their own individual portfolios and trades.

Some of these institutional investors are critically important in specific types of countries. For example, those countries which are oil rich and exporting nations generally contain one or more massive sovereign wealth funds which possess a lion's share of the investable wealth of the nation. These are usually government controlled and administered institutional funds and investors.

They can amass even hundreds of billions of investable dollars, as have the Norwegian, Abu Dhabi, Saudi Arabian, Qatari, and Kuwaiti funds. In developed nations, it is the pension funds and insurance companies which control a substantial portion of the excess and readily deployable and investable capital.

Investor

Strictly speaking, an investor is any person or entity that makes an investment. In the past, the word investors has acquired a far more specific meaning. In the world of business and finance, investors has come to characterize those individuals or companies that routinely buy debt instruments like bonds, or equity issues like stocks in an attempt to make financial profits. They hope to realize such gains in return for financing or providing capital to a company that is looking to expand.

Investors also relates to other types of individuals, businesses, or parties that put money into different types of investments. Although this is a less commonly used version of the word investors, it can relate to those engaging in currency, real estate, commodities, derivatives, or other personal property investments like art or antiques. An example of this would be a real estate investor. They purchase a piece of property or a house with the hopes of selling it for a greater amount of money than for what they purchased it. Similarly, commodities' investors are hoping to buy contracts or options on hard assets like gold, oil, or lumber cheaply to sell them later more dearly.

Investors are commonly buying such stocks, bonds, or other types of assets and holding on to them with the goal of realizing one of two types of returns, or in some unusual cases both types. These are capital gains or cash flow investments. Investors who are interested in capital gains are simply looking to sell an instrument or asset that they obtained at one price for a greater amount. When they do this, they realize a capital gain. Should they sell the investment for less than they purchased it, they would instead realize a capital loss. Capital gains can only be realized one time on an investment, as the investors will have sold the investment and have to look for another investment to begin the process anew once again.

Cash flow investors are alternatively looking for a repetitive income stream. They hope to achieve regular, smaller sums of passive income just from holding their investment. Dividends on a stock, royalties on an oil or gas investment, and rents from a residential or commercial realty property are all examples of cash flow investments and returns. So long as the investor owns the cash flow investment, he or she should be able to continuously count on a regular income stream.

The word investor commonly gives the connotation of a person who acquires these assets for the longer term. This stands in contrast to a day trader or even short term investor. Investors can be professional or self taught amateurs.

Investors also represent many entities other than individuals or even traditional businesses. They can be investment groups like clubs, venture capital investors who provide money to start up companies, investment banks, investment trusts such as REIT Real Estate Investment Trusts, hedge funds and mutual funds, and even sovereign wealth funds that invest on behalf of their respective nations.

IRA Custodian

An IRA custodian is commonly represented by some form of a financial institution. This would likely be a brokerage or a bank. These Individual Retirement Accounts' custodians have the job of protecting your assets in your IRA.

Per the rules of the Internal Revenue Service, such IRA custodians have to be financial institutions that are approved. People can not choose to perform the role of an IRA custodian. In order for institutions that are not financial in nature to perform the responsibilities of such IRA custodians, they have to receive a special approval issued to them by the Internal Revenue Service.

These IRA Custodians actually carry out the transactions that the clients request of them. They also file any and all reports, maintain all required records of anything done on the account as a custodian, and send out statements and notices for taxes, either of which may be mandated by law or the agreement for custodianship.

They sometimes will disburse the assets found in the IRA as per the wishes of the client, as well as file all necessary and relevant paper work with this action. One thing that IRA custodians do not have to do is to offer legal or investment advice to you, the IRA holder. This means that you have to provide the custodian of your IRA with clear and accurate instructions which follow the code established by the IRS.

IRA custodians can be responsible for overseeing a great range of investment securities and financial instruments. While IRS rules restrict IRA money being invested into collectibles like rare coins and artworks, or even life insurance, the custodian is able to work with various different investments like franchises, real estate, tax liens, and mortgages.

Still, a great number of financial institutions acting as IRA custodians will choose to restrict the kinds of investments that they will allow to be held in one of their IRA's under custodianship. It is important for owners of IRA's who wish to have their funds placed into investments that are not traditional for IRA's, such as real estate or franchises, to seek out and choose an IRA custodian who will allow and work with these kinds of investments. This is the particular reason that a real estate management firm might choose to attain IRS certification in order to obtain the permission for overseeing real estate investment IRA's.

Much of the time, IRA customers will just deposit their retirement money and assets into their account that the custodian holds and will supply them with overall guidelines for their investments. The IRS mandates fiduciary responsibility for IRA custodians. They have to place clients' interests first. This translates to practical requirements, such as not being allowed to put the IRA money into investments and projects that come with a great amount of risk, unless they have the customer's expressed consent.

IRA custodians are also involved with self directed IRA's. Self directed IRA's contain investments that are actively managed directly by the customer. The custodian only performs the actions that the customer requests in these cases.

Keogh Plan

Keogh Plans are like 401(k) plans intended for small businesses. They are distinguished from them by having higher limits than the 401(k)s do. These tax deferred pension plans can be established by businesses that are not incorporated or individuals who are self employed.

These types of plans can be one of three types. There are money purchase plans preferred by those who are high income earners. Profit sharing plans provide yearly flexibility that is dependent on the company profits. Defined benefit plans feature higher yearly minimums.

Keogh Plans are also referred to as HR(10) plans. They are permitted to invest in the same investments as IRAs and 401(k)s. This includes stocks and bonds, annuities, and certificates of deposit. The reasons these plans are so popular for sole proprietors and small business owners has to do with their higher contribution limits. A downside to them revolves around their greater maintenance costs and more burdensome administration than SEP Simplified Employee Pension plans feature.

These Keogh Plans derive their name from the creator of the concept Eugene Keogh. He put together the 1962 Self Employed Individuals Tax Retirement Act which became named for him. The plans received a name change after the Economic Growth and Tax Relief Reconciliation Act passed in 2001. This act so altered these plans that the IRS code dropped the reference name of Keogh.

They simply call them HR(10) plans now. These retirement accounts are still utilized, but have lost many followers to the solo 401(k) and the SEP IRA. The HR(10) plans still find a good fit with professionals who are highly compensated as with lawyers or dentists who are self employed. Otherwise these plans generally do not serve retirement savers better than the competing plans.

The HR(10) plans come in two different principal breakdowns. These are defined contribution and defined benefit plans. With defined contribution plans, self employed persons can decide the amount of contribution they will make every year. This can be done either through money purchase or profit sharing plans.

Money purchase requires that the profits percentage to go in the Keogh be decided at the beginning of the year. If the employed person makes profits, these contributions must be made without changes or a penalty will be assessed by the IRS. The amounts owners contribute to their profit sharing plans may be changed every year. As much as 25% of income can be deducted and contributed every year. The limit on this amount is $53,000 for 2015 and 2016.

Defined benefit plans operate much as traditional pensions would. Business owners determine a pension goal for themselves then fund it. As much as $210,000 may be contributed in a year (up to 100% of all compensation) for the years 2015 and 2016. Business owners make all contributions in both types of Keogh plans as pre-tax. This means they these contributions come out of the taxable salary before taxes are figured.

Keoghs plans are also similar to typical 401(k)s in the way that invested monies are able to be tax deferred until retirement. This may start as early as 59 ½ years old but can not be delayed until any later than 70 years of age. Any withdrawals taken before these years are federally and potentially state taxed as regular income and also penalized at 10%. Exceptions to the penalty rules exist if certain physical or financial health issues come up for the account owner before retirement.

In order to maintain a Keogh Plan, a great amount of paperwork has to be filed each year. This includes the Form 5500 from the IRS. It requires a financial professional or tax accountant's help.

Lloyds Banking Group

Lloyds Banking Group represents the biggest financial services consortium in the United Kingdom. As a financial services provider that concentrates on business and retail clients, they count millions of customers throughout the country. They have a presence in practically every community of the U.K.

Part of the impressive size and strength of Lloyds Banking Group centers on its major household name brands. Among the most important of these are Lloyds Bank, Bank of Scotland, Halifax, and Scottish Widows.

The main businesses of the Lloyds Banking Group help it to touch so many customers in their daily lives. They provide retail, business, and corporate banking. The group also delivers general and life insurance. They provide investment opportunities and pension plans as well.

The shares of the Lloyds Banking Group trade on the London Stock Exchange as well as the New York Stock Exchange. The company is one of the biggest in the main British stock market benchmark index the FTSE 100. It also ranks among the largest banks in the world.

Lloyds Banking Group also runs the biggest retail bank in the United Kingdom. This was formerly known as Lloyds TSB but is now simply called Lloyds Bank. It claims the highest number of bank branches in the country. This gives them access to a diversified and massive base of customers. It helps them to cross sell products and services so that they are able to offer a total package of financial services and products for their clients. Their mobile, telephone, and digital services are comprehensive.

The history of this leading member in the Lloyds Banking Group, Lloyds Bank, goes back three centuries. Founded in 1765, the bank celebrated its 250 year anniversary back in 2015. This also makes it among the oldest of the largest banks in the world.

Lloyds Bank started its first branch in Birmingham where it operated as a single branch for a hundred years. In the twentieth century, it pursued decades of mergers to grow into first a national and then an international bank. The 1995 merger with TSB changed its name to Lloyds TSB Bank for a time. In the process of its expansion, the bank gained control of the company which invented Travelers Checks, opened the first British ATM machine, and had a foremost part in launching among the first credit cards in the United Kingdom.

Bank of Scotland is headquartered in Edinburgh. It turns out to be the oldest bank in Scotland. The Scottish Parliament founded it in 1695. It has remained a cornerstone of Scottish business since the act created it. The Parliament originally established the bank to increase the trade of Scotland with nearby trading partners. These included neighboring England and the Low Countries (now Belgium, the Netherlands, and Luxembourg).

The Bank of Scotland also claims a number of pioneering firsts in the industry. It became the very first European commercial bank to issue banknotes with success. It continues to do this today. The bank became the first in the U.K. to put in a computer for processing accounts in 1959. In 2009 the bank joined the Lloyds Group.

The banking group also owns the Halifax brand. This is a building society that arose in 1852. A little group set it up in meetings at the Halifax based Old Cock Inn. They created this investment and loan society to benefit the area working people. Individuals with extra money were able to invest it while others could borrow these funds to build or buy their own house. Eventually Halifax grew into the largest building society around the globe. It counts over 18 million customers today.

Merrill Lynch

Merrill Lynch proves to be the global markets and commercial banking operations of Bank of American Corporation and all of its various affiliates around the world. They offer the largest network of bank branches in the United States.

Among their national customer base are more than 47 million individual, business, corporate, and institutional accounts. This means that nearly one out of every six Americans is a customer of the banking group. The bank also counts operations in over 35 countries around the globe. The U.S. based bank is commonly listed as the 10th largest bank in the world.

The global footprint of Bank of America Merrill Lynch permits them to provide financial services and products to investors, consumers, and businesses in all regions of the earth. They organize their global operations in over 35 countries in the four proprietary groups of Europe, the Middle East, and Africa; Latin America; Asia Pacific; and the Americas.

The most important presence the bank has outside of North America lies in the Europe, Middle East, and Africa group. This EMEA division includes operations in 32 cities spanning 23 countries on the three continents. Bank of America Merrill Lynch has been partnering with European markets since the end of the First World War in the year 1922.

They maintain over 14,000 staff members in the EMEA. These personnel, branches, and offices provide financial products and services for individual, business, institutional, corporate, and government customers through their knowledge of the international markets combined with a superior local market understanding.

In Latin America, Merrill Lynch is proud to advise both institutional investors and corporations spanning the range of Latin America. They have effectively served this market for over 30 years. The group maintains offices or branches in seven nations where they deliver insights into a range of regulatory and market scenarios. The bank is a significant operator in the countries of Brazil, Mexico, and Chile.

The Asia Pacific group of Merrill Lynch provides 12 different Asian nations and territories across over a dozen languages in five different time zones with over 60 years of regionally based experience.

Though it boasts a significant and growing international presence, the true core strength and locations of Merrill Lynch have always been and likely always will remain in the Americas, particularly in the U.S. and Canada. Here it offers individuals a broad and impressive range of consumer and investment services. Consumer services include checking and savings accounts, credit cards, and home loans.

Under the flagship brands of both Merrill Lynch Wealth Management and U.S. Trust, the group provides individuals with wealth management services through its network of over 18,000 client assisting financial planner representatives (as of 2015). These services they deliver include wealth management banking, investment management, concentrated stock strategies, wealth transfers, trusts, tax and estate planning, retirement services, insurance services, and philanthropic management.

They offer their millions of business and corporate accounts in the United States and Canada a wide range of services through Bank of America and its various subsidiaries. These include lending and company financing, capital advisory and raising services, merchant services, card solutions, fraud prevention, payments and receivables management, liquidity management, equipment finance and leasing, investment management and products, retirement and benefit planning services, trade services, mergers and acquisitions, commodity, currency, and interest rate management, and philanthropic management.

Merrill Lynch also serves institutional clients in the U.S. and Canada. It boasts of leveraged performance in asset management on a global scale. Their services portfolio is both broadly comprehensive and sophisticated. It includes research that leads the industry and expertise in multiple industries and regions of the globe.

Money Market Funds

Money market funds are investment vehicles with a unique objective of keeping a consistent NAV net asset value of $1 each share while they provide interest for their investing share holders. To accomplish this, the portfolio of a money market fund is made up of securities that are short term in nature with maturities which are under a year. These securities typically are liquid debt and money instruments that are of the highest quality. Investors can easily buy money market fund shares by going through banks, brokerage firms, or mutual funds directly.

The ultimate goal of these money market funds is to give their investors a safe haven investment for assets which are both readily accessible and equivalent to cash. In essence they are mutual funds. Among their most common characteristics are that they offer low returns and provide low risk as an investment.

Because these funds offer comparatively lower returns than many other investments, financial advisors recommend that investors not remain in these vehicles as a long term selection. Their returns will not provide sufficient appreciation on capital in order to achieve the investors' objectives over a longer time frame. Employer provided retirement plans will often sweep employees' unallocated dollars into these funds until they give orders as to where to invest them specifically.

The pros to money market funds can be significant. They offer more than simply high liquidity and lower risk. A number of investors find them appealing because there are not any fund entrance or exit fees (or loads) as with many mutual funds. A variety of them will offer investors gains which have tax advantages. These come from investments they make in state and federally tax exempt municipal securities. Other investments which these funds could hold include T-bills and other shorter time frame government debt issues, corporate commercial paper, and CDs certificates of deposit.

There are also some downsides to money market funds besides their low returns. Though they are supposed to be stable and consistent in their values, they are not insured by the FDIC Federal Deposit Insurance

Corporation. This means that in the rare cases where such funds break the buck, investors can suffer losses of principal. Competing investments like CDs, savings accounts, and money market deposits accounts provide similar returns but do offer this government backed guarantee of principal. This does not stop investors from regarding money market funds as extremely safe. The funds are carefully regulated by the Investment Company Act of 1940.

The government changed the rules on such money market funds regarding their net asset values and in what they could invest in 2014. After that year, the funds were not permitted to set their NAV permanently at $1 any longer. They did this because of the three times in the history of such funds where the $1 share price had been broken (as of 2016). It had created "bank runs" on the assets of the money market funds in 2008 when it occurred most recently in the Financial Crisis.

The American SEC Securities and Exchange Commission decided to prevent this from happening again by changing the fund management rules to provide them with more resilience and better stability. Such new restrictions more strictly limited the assets these funds were allowed to hold. The SEC also introduced triggers that would suspend redemptions and charge liquidity fees to prevent chaos in the markets. The fund managers had to start utilizing a floating NAV which created risk where it was not perceived to exist previously. Individual investors were not impacted by the floating NAV share rule since the funds are designated as retail funds and are exempt from this rule.

Money Purchase Plan

Money Purchase Plans are another type of retirement vehicle that some traditional for profit companies offer their employees. In these plans, employees and their employers both make contributions. These contributions from the employers are figured from a yearly earnings percentage.

The plans are different from Profit Sharing Plans in which the annual basis of profitability determines how large the contributions are. Money Purchase Plans' annual earnings percentages assigned for contributions stay the same ever year as set out in the originals terms of the retirement benefit plan. These plans do not enjoy a great deal of attention from the media. Despite this they are still a critical employer provided retirement vehicle that offers significant tax advantages for employees.

These plans are classified as defined contribution plans much like 401(k)s, even though the employer contributions are mandatory. Employees enjoy account control over the investments as much as the specific plan investment rules permit. Account owners also carry full responsibility for determining when any money is distributed or transferred.

The beauty of these Money Purchase Plans is that every contribution made to them is fully tax deductible while all gains in the account are tax deferred. This means the accounts are funded with pretax dollars. None of the money in the account will become taxable until it is distributed at retirement. The maximum contributions to the accounts in a year from employer and employee are $53,000 for 2016.

There are some downsides to the Money Purchase Plans. A significant one is that the retirement accounts require substantial administration costs for these types of accounts. This comes out of the account returns and earnings on investments. Besides this, account holders are unable to obtain loans from these types of plans. Most other defined contribution plans do allow for such loans to be taken. Rollovers can also be hard to accomplish with these types of plans. The level of difficulty depends on the individual guidelines of a specific plan.

It is critical for anyone considering a rollover to investigate the particular documents of the plan. The IRS does not limit rollovers from these plans. It is instead the specifics of the plans themselves that make it difficult for those who are still working for the company and under the official retirement age to transfer them. When the plan allows for them, rollovers proceed as with any other qualified retirement vehicle. They can be transferred into an individual IRA or rolled into another employer 401(k) plan.

Any individuals who attempt to take cash distributions before they reach the government set retirement age of 59 ½ will suffer substantial penalties. Besides becoming fully taxable, these funds will be subjected to the 10% early withdrawal IRS penalty. Because of the stiff penalties, direct rollovers are more sensible than indirect ones.

When individuals begin indirect rollovers, they receive a check distribution. The 60 day clock to complete the rollover then begins ticking. There are also withholding requirements when these types of indirect rollovers are attempted. Early distribution penalties can result from not completing these rollovers according to the strict IRS timetable.

Investment choices are a weak point of these Money Purchase Plans. Legally they are allowed to invest in individual government and corporate bonds and stocks, mutual funds, options, and exchange traded fund shares. The plan provider may limit these choices further as they see fit.

This means that these accounts may not invest in physical gold bullion holdings directly as with self directed or precious metals IRAs. They can participate in paper gold investments such as gold mining company stocks or mutual funds that own them. They may also purchase gold mining ETFs or gold ETFs like GLD.

MyRA Account

MyRA Account is a new form of retirement plan that the government set up under the auspices of the U.S. Department of the Treasury. They intended it for workers who do not have access to any other form of retirement plan through their workplace and who do not have a convenient vehicle of their own for saving for retirement. It is a Roth IRA and is governed by the Roth IRA rules.

It offers several advantages other forms of retirement accounts do not. There are no fees or costs to set it up or maintain it. The account is automatically invested in a government Treasury fund and pays the simple rate, so there are not any complex investment options or decisions to make. Because it is based in Treasuries of the United States government, there is no risk of losing any money. The Obama administration created and issued this MyRA account plan in 2015.

As with other types of retirement plans and accounts, participants are able to set up automatic payroll contributions to this account. When they change jobs to work for a different company, the account stays with them as it is their own personal retirement account.

The accounts also provide the distinctive advantage in allowing participants to take out the money they placed in the MyRA account whenever they wish. There is no additional tax levied or penalties assessed at any point when they do this. This means that there is no early withdrawal penalty associated with the MyRA accounts, making it more like a savings account than a government approved retirement plan.

Participants in the MyRA Account like that their money is invested in safe U.S. government Treasuries. The investment is fully backed by the United States Treasury. They state that the account will earn (with no risk) an interest rate of 1.5% APR for the month of July 2016. This is based on the Government Securities Fund. This particular fund earned a 2015 average return of 2.04% and a 2.94% average annual return in the ten year period that concluded in December of 2015.

As a starter retirement account, the MyRA account provides the unmatched benefit of no charges to set up or open it and no ongoing maintenance fees for account owners. It also allows savers to contribute any amount they like with no minimum, even $2 contributions. The investments grow with the same tax advantages as a Roth IRA with after tax dollars. This means that the interest and principle will not be taxable when it is withdrawn from the account at any point between now and through retirement.

The MyRA account does come with maximum contribution limits as do all types of retirement savings vehicles. For tax years 2015 and 2016, participants may contribute no more than $5,500 in the year. If they are older than 49 years of age, this amount increases to $6,500 for the year in catch up contribution amounts which the IRS permits. Besides the annual contribution limit amounts, there are also the same lifetime contribution limits that apply to standard Roth IRA accounts.

Critics of this account have warned that this plan represents an all too easy mark and tempting target for the U.S. government if it runs into financing troubles. In the event that Treasury needs ready to access funds, it would not be able to find any that were easier to seize than the ones it is holding itself on behalf of American account holders. They also accuse the government of setting up a plan that props up and creates demand for Treasuries using Americans' retirement funds as the vehicle to do this.

Net Worth

Net worth is a figure that represents a business, an individual, or another group's difference between the assets that they have and the liabilities that they owe. Figuring up this net worth is done by first taking all of the entity's debts and obligations and then subtracting that number from the entire sum of assets. If the total of all of these assets is greater than the sum of all of the debts and obligations, then a positive net worth results. Otherwise, when the debts are greater than the assets, then the entity has a negative net worth.

When you sit down to determine the net worth figure, every asset should be totaled in the operation. There are many different kinds of assets. These are comprised of cash in the bank, holdings of stocks, real estate, bonds, and other types of investments, and major possessions like vehicles. Correctly figuring out the different assets' values is done with the use of the up to date fair market value, not the cost paid for the item when it is purchased.

You must also correctly add up the total of debts and obligations when you are attempting to get a correct net worth value. Liabilities cover many different obligations, like a car payment, mortgage, total of credit card debt outstanding, and any other forms of loans that have balances left on them. Both every asset and liability must be measured in order to come up with an accurate net worth.

Knowing your present net worth is very useful and meaningful. If you are able to cover all of your outstanding debt obligations simply by selling of all of your assets, then you have a financial condition that is fairly stable and in order. If your assets are more than sufficient to cover all of your obligations, then your finances are in greater shape. Most businesses and people seek to reach a point that they have actual positive net worth.

There are a few benefits from having a correct understanding of your net worth. It is essential that your present assets' value is greater than your present debt load. A person who owes more money than they actually own presents a profile of a person who is not an especially good credit risk. Without a positive net worth, many lending institutions like banks will think twice about providing you with the most advantageous loan rates offered. This is because they feel that you present more of a risk to lend money.

It is also good to know where your net worth stands because it is a helpful beginning point for your general financial planning. Should you discover that you hardly have sufficient assets with which to cover your present amount of debts, then this is a good sign that you should not engage in any other purchases until later, after you have eliminated several of your debts. This means that if you occasionally figure up your net worth, then you will comprehend not only where you stand now, but also when you will be in a better position to purchase a new car.

New Deal

The New Deal represented a new domestic economic program that American President Franklin D. Roosevelt put into place in the years from 1933 to 1939.

The goals of this extensive program were to provide immediate and urgent economic relief to the unemployed along with much needed economic reforms in finance, agriculture, industry, labor, waterpower, and housing. These economic programs and reforms massively grew the scope of the federal government's role. The term actually came from the Democratic nomination acceptance speech of Roosevelt on July 2, 1932.

American voters had reacted forcefully to the unhelpful responses of President Herbert Hoover's administration in dealing with the devastation brought on by the Great Depression. The American electorate massively turned out to vote for the democratic candidate's pledge of creating a new deal for the country's forgotten man.

The New Deal stood in contrast to the general American political and economic ideas of laissez faire capitalism. Instead it brought in an economy regulated and participated in by the government. The goal was to bring harmony to economic interests that conflicted.

The Hundred Days initial several months period of Roosevelt's first term saw a great amount of the New Deal laws passed. His first goal was to help out the enormous groups of unemployed workers and to ease their suffering. He did this with his government entities the CCC Civilian Conservation Corps and the WPA Works Progress Administration. They provided short term emergency government assistance to the unemployed and offered construction project employment, temporary work, and youth employment in the national parks and forests.

In the years leading up to 1935 the New Deal also aimed to restore the devastated agricultural and business communities. Roosevelt gave authority to the National Recovery Administration to encourage lost industrial activity. They could propose industrial codes that oversaw wages, trade practices, child labor, hours, and labor union collective bargaining.

The New Deal made efforts to oversee the financial organizations so that there would not be repeats of the widespread bank failures and the catastrophic 1929 stock market crash.

It created the SEC Securities and Exchange Commission in order to safeguard investors from deceptive investment marketing and sales. Bank deposits became insured by the new government insurance agency the FDIC Federal Deposit Insurance Corporation. All banks could become members of the Federal Reserve System under this program.

The agenda also addressed farming and electrical power. The AAA Agricultural Adjustment Administration tried to raise the rates paid to farmers by giving them subsidies in order to produce the key staple crops. In 1933 the government founded the TVA Tennessee Valley Authority to deliver less expensive electricity and better navigation as well as to produce nitrates and stop floods. This covered seven states and made major improvements for Americans who lived in these areas.

By 1935 the New Deal had moved on to help out working Americans living in the cities. Labor unions were substantially strengthened by the 1935 Wagner Act. This also gave the federal government more power in determining industrial relations as it founded the NLRB National Labor Relations Board to run the program. Forgotten homeowners received aid as well. Congress passed laws that helped refinance on the edge mortgages. Bank loans were also guaranteed for mortgages and for modernizing homes.

The most substantial and lasting programs of the New Deal had to do with retirement and unemployment benefits. In 1935 and 1939 it established Social Security. This delivered benefits to the elderly and widows. It also provided disability insurance and unemployment compensation to those out of work. In 1938, minimum wages became established alongside maximum working hours in specific industries.

Offshore Bonds

Offshore Bonds are sometimes called offshore investment bonds. These investment vehicles allow individuals to gain control over what point they pay tax, to whom they will pay such tax, and how much they will ultimately pay in the end. These types of bonds are offered internationally from some of the mega global multinational life insurance firms like Britain's Old Mutual International and Friends Provident International, Genarali Worldwide, RL360, and Zurich International.

Such Offshore Bonds would not ever be domiciled in the United Kingdom or the United States. Rather they would be based in such offshore tax havens as Luxembourg, Guernsey in the Channel Islands, or the Isle of Man. More and more these days, international expatriates choose Dublin, Ireland for a domicile for these investments. This is because of the perception that Ireland offers tax efficiency and effective regulatory protection.

When money like this is not brought back into most countries (beside the United States) where the citizen is from in the form of either capital appreciation or income, then it will not be subject to those jurisdictions' taxes. This is why investors have to consider the tax jurisdiction where they are residents when they cash out their Offshore Bond. It means that selecting the best location and provider of the bond is extremely critical, since this will determine which access and taxation rules apply in the event of a cash out scenario.

A great number of the Offshore Bonds prove to be inexpensive, completely transparent, and tax efficient planning investment vehicles. Investors still have to be careful that they are not abusing this type of tax and investment vehicle. Reality is that whether a bond is offshore or onshore, it truly is an investment masquerading as an insurance contract. This delivers to the investors an array of some helpful tax benefits.

There are a number of good reasons for why investors (and especially those who are not U.S. citizens who can not escape from their own taxing regime the IRS no matter where they live unless they give up their citizenship) utilize such investment vehicles as Offshore Bonds. For starters, an offshore bond will not be considered an income generating asset. Because of this truth, trustees and individuals do not have to fill in any tax returns which require self assessment.

Income which is reinvested in the Offshore Bonds will not produce income tax events. These bonds have advantages over pensions and retirement accounts as well, since investors can assign them to another individual or legal entity at will. Money kept inside of the bond may be switched around and still will not require any Capital Gains Tax payment or even tax reporting situations.

There are similarly income tax-free events with these Offshore Bonds. It is possible to draw out as much as five percent of the premium originally deposited or paid without creating any taxing liability. This can be done over a span of 20 consecutive years. When owners make their five percent withdrawals, this is not an income-generating event, but instead simply a return of original capital to the bond holder. These bonds may also be put inside of a trust and then removed from it without creating an income taxing event.

Without a doubt, these Offshore Bonds have proven to be enormously popular with expatriates living abroad. They provide tremendous possible tax advantages for anyone who will reside outside of their native country (besides for citizens of the U.S.). The reason for this is that investors are able to claim tax relief for those gains which they make when residing offshore. This significant benefit is known as time apportionment relief.

For British residents as an example, they are able to lower the tax which must be paid commiserate with the amount of time they resided outside of the United Kingdom. So if they were bondholding residents of Spain for half the life of holding the bond, then this would lower the amount of taxes they had to pay for any income or gains in Britain by half.

The danger of course is that some commission-based financial advisors will try to take advantage of the investors in this type of program. When they are not correctly established with extreme transparency, the unscrupulous financial advisor may draw out a significant amount of the savings percentage wise. This transfer of wealth is not illegal, as it is merely a case of high fees and commissions. These Offshore Bonds can be dangerously opaque if investors are not careful.

Passive Income

Passive income refers to money that, once it is arranged and established, does not require additional work from the person getting it. A variety of different types of passive income exist. Among them are movie, music, book, screenplay, television, and patent royalties. Other samples of passive income include click through income, rental income, and revenue from online advertising.

Activities that lead to passive income have something in common. They usually need a great amount of money, time, or both invested in them upfront to get them started. There are financial means to establishing passive income as well. You could purchase a rental property or choose to invest in a partnership or other form of company where you are a silent partner. The income that you derive from these investment activities is deemed to be passive.

Various other kinds of passive income do not need a great deal of financial investment made in them, but instead require great amounts of effort, time, and even creativity to achieve. More than a year can be required to either build up a popular website that can contribute passive income from advertising or to write a great novel. Making money from such passive income that is actually profit may take longer.

Books are a good example of how long it can take to actually make money from passive income. Publishers generally get to recover all of their printing and promoting costs, as well as any advance monies given to authors, before royalties are created and paid. Books that sell poorly could turn out to pay the author little to nothing.

Websites have a different set of challenges for their creators. There has to be more than simply good content to make money from them. They must similarly rank high in the search engine results for the necessary amount of visitors to find and go to the website. Unless a great number of visitor hits are recorded on a website, the passive income that is generated will be negligible or even none.

People are willing to put in such a huge amount of time with little assurance of results because they know that the passive income generating activity will create money for them around the clock for years to come, if it is successful. This means that passive income money is constantly being made, even when the person is asleep or on vacation. If you are able to get one passive income project up and running well, then you can attempt others. This way, you might hope to develop a few different income streams that result in a significant annual revenue which can even support you.

Many investors believe that passive income is the most superior kind that you can achieve. This is why rental properties can be so popular. Even though they can require a significant amount of maintenance work and tenant management, they can provide substantial income once several such properties are owned and made profitable.

Pension Benefit Guaranty Corporation (PBGC)

Pension Benefit Guaranty Corporation is also referred to many times by its government given acronym the PBGC. This federal agency arose as a result of the ERISA Employee Retirement Income Security Act of 1974. Its mission is to safeguard the benefits of pensions provided by private sector benefit plans that are defined. These plans commonly promise to pay out a fixed amount per month when retirement begins.

Should a plan end in the event of plan termination, and there not be enough money to pay out all of the promised benefits, then the insurance program of the Pension Benefit Guaranty Corporation will pay out the pension plan-provided benefit to the limits which the law establishes. This means that the majority of plan participants will actually still get the full benefit which they had already earned and been promised before termination of the plan occurred.

Some people have wondered where the money for the PBGC comes from so that they can cover failed plan benefits this way. The answer is that those firms whose plans the Pension Benefit Guaranty Corporation protects are required to pay insurance premiums for the insurance. PBGC similarly has investments as well as seized assets that they assume when they become trustee of a terminated pension plan. They also have assets from recoveries of firms which used to manage the plans. They do not derive any of this benefit-covering money from the general tax base. Even if a given employer does not pay its insurance premiums properly into the fund, the defined benefits pension plan will still be insured.

Employers may close out these defined benefit plans in what the PBGC calls a standard termination. They are only allowed to do this once they have demonstrated that the plan is sufficiently capitalized to pay out all owed benefits to the plan participants. To do this, the plan will be required to do one of two things. They might buy an annuity off of an insurance company. This annuity will pay out the promised lifelong benefits upon retirement of the participants.

Alternatively, they may provide one time single large payments that amount to the full benefit value amount. The PBGC provided guarantee of the plan will then cease to exist once the employer either buys this annuity or provides the beneficiaries of the plan with the one time, single payment.

Should the plan lack the money needed to cover all promised pension benefits to the participants of the plan while the employing firm finds itself in financial trouble, then the employers are able to request a distress termination from the PBGC fund. The plan will only be terminated under these scenarios when the employing firm proves to either a bankruptcy court or the PBGC itself that they will not be able to continue operating the firm if the plan does not become terminated. Once such an application request is approved, the PBGC typically becomes trustee and administrator of the plan. They would then pay out the promised plan benefits to the extent allowed by law.

The law similarly allows the Pension Benefit Guaranty Corporation to act alone in order to close out a pension plan where necessary to safeguard the participants' interests or that of the insurance program of the PBGC itself. As a standard procedural example, they will terminate any plan that is sure to be incapable of paying out the promised benefits when they become due.

The PBGC covers the overwhelming majority of defined benefit plans which private sector businesses provide. The lion's share pledge to pay out a set benefit (typically in a once per month distribution) upon commencement of the beneficiaries' retirement. Some pledge to deliver a single-value lump sum payment for their benefit. It is important to know that the PBGC will never insure any defined contribution plans that do not pledge to deliver a guaranteed benefit amount.

PBGC insures defined benefit plans offered by private-sector employers. Most promise to pay a specified benefit, usually a monthly amount, at retirement. Others, including cash-balance plans, may state the promised benefit as a single value. PBGC does not insure defined contribution plans, which are retirement plans that do not promise specific benefit amounts, such as profit-sharing or 401(k) plans.

PBGC does not commonly insure any plans that lawyers and doctors offer if they have under 25 active participants. They also do not cover the plans provided by local, state, or Federal governments. Finally, church group pension plans will not be covered.

Pension Entitlements

Pension entitlements are the monies that have been promised to employees who are guaranteed a pension by the company for which they work. The majority of newly issued pensions anymore come from Federal, state, and local government employees. Some companies still offer pension entitlements to their employees who serve a minimum number of years with the firm, such as from twenty to thirty years.

These companies are becoming fewer and farther between as more and more corporations switch over to matching 401K retirement plans that cost them far less money and entail significantly lesser liabilities every year. This is because with pre set limit matches to 401K contributions, companies can know for certain how much money they will have to come out of pocket, whereas with pensions, it has much to do with how long the retirees live.

Pension entitlements are at risk as they become larger every year. Many companies are struggling to keep up with their pension entitlements as their retiring employees live longer and longer. Because of the danger to failing pensions that many retirees count on, the PBGC was set up. This entity acronym stands for Pension Benefit Guarantee Corporation.

The government created this entity in the Employee Retirement Income Security Act in 1974. Today, it safe guards in excess of forty-four million American retirees and workers pensions, covering the pension entitlements against default from the companies underlying them. These are held in greater than twenty-nine thousand multi employer and private single employer defined benefit pension plans.

The PBGC does not derive money from the general tax revenues in protecting the pension entitlements. Insurance premiums that Congress sets are paid by the sponsors of defined benefit plans, assets from pension plans that PBGC trustees, investment income of the PBGC, and recoveries made from companies who are no longer handling their own plans.

As a result of the financial crisis of 2007-2010, many private pension funds have suffered disastrous losses. In 2008 alone, this amounted to tangible losses of in excess of twenty-six percent. Even though the markets recovered somewhat, many pension funds had locked in their losses by selling the underwater investments. As a result of these terrible financial events, even more pension entitlements in the United States are now under funded.

In order to help make up for these, businesses will have to make substantially larger contributions in the future. It remains to be seen if the Pension Benefit Guarantee Corporation will be able to keep up with and cover all of the unfunded pension entitlements that have been promised to retirees and workers. Some experts have speculated that the PBGC itself will require bailouts in the hundreds of billions of dollars in the near future.

Pension Funds

Pension funds are retirement plans which mandate that an employer must do contributions for the benefit of their employee's future. They contribute such money into a pool of funds. This pool then becomes invested for the employee's benefit. All earnings which the investments make accrue to the workers once they reach retirement.

Besides these mandatory contributions, there are pension plans which have components of voluntary contributions. Pension plans can permit workers to contribute a portion of their wages and income into the investment plan to help prepare for their retirement. It is also customary and encouraged for an employer to match some part of the yearly contributions of the employees. The limitations on this amount which they can contribute by matching funds are set by the Internal Revenue Service or IRS.

Two primary kinds of pension funds exist today. With defined benefit plans, the companies promise their staff will obtain a minimum benefit amount when they retire. These kinds of plans deliver the minimum regardless of how poorly the investment pool that underlies the fund actually performs. This means that the employer will be required to make a particular pension payment guarantee for their retired employees in these cases.

There is a formula that determines the precise amount It is typically built on the combination of years in service and aggregate earnings. In the cases where the pension plan assets are insufficient to pay out the defined and guaranteed minimum benefits, then it is the firm which will have to make up the balance of the minimum payment.

Such employer sponsored pension plans and pension funds in the United States hail from the decade of the 1870s. At their peak in the roaring 1980s, they amounted to a participation rate of almost 50 percent of the total workers in the private sector. Around 90 percent of all public employees as well as approximately 10 percent of the private ones receive the coverage of this kind of defined benefits plan nowadays.

The second type of pension funds are defined contribution plans. With these, the employing company engages in particular set contributions to the retirement plans of their employees. They typically will match to some degree their employees' contributions to the plan. The ultimate payouts which the staff receive while retired come down to the investment results of the plan. In these cases, the firms which sponsor them do not have additional minimum payout liability after they make their pre-set contributions.

The reason these are so much more popular now is that they prove to be far less costly for employers than do traditional forms of pensions. This is because companies are not backing whatever benefits the funds are unable to produce. More and more private corporations and firms have moved over to this form of plan and have closed out their defined benefit plans. While there are a number of defined contribution plans, the 401(k) plan is the most well-known one. For the benefit of not for profit workers, the equivalent plan turns out to be the 403(b) plan.

When the phrase is utilized, "pension plan" typically refers to these more traditional forms of defined benefit plans. These payouts remain established, controlled, and ultimately funded 100 percent by the sponsoring employer. There are corporations which provide a choice from both plan types. Some will even permit their workers to roll over their 401(k) plan balances to their defined benefit or "pension" plans.

A final version of these is the pay as you go pension plan. Employers set these up themselves. Such plans are entirely funded during the accumulation phase by the workers. They may choose to make either a lump sum contribution (as with an annuity) or regular salary-deducted contributions. Besides these capabilities, such plans prove remarkably similar to other 401(k) plans. One disadvantage to them is that they lack a company matching participation program.

Personal Assets

Personal assets are items of value that belong to an individual. There are many examples of such tangible personal assets. Among these are houses, real estate, cars, and jewelry. Personal assets can also be any other thing with cash value.

When individuals go to a bank or other institution to apply for loans, such personal assets and their values are often considered. These assets are also the bedrock of the formula for net worth for consumers. The value of people's personal assets can be higher than they expect and surprise them as so many different items can be included under this label.

There are many personal assets that are material and easy to measure. These include such financial assets as savings accounts, checking accounts, and retirement accounts. Assets that have a value that can not be easily accessed are also included in the personal assets category. This includes life insurance policies and annuities that have cash values. Other items of value which would be included in a list of personal assets cover such items as antiques, art collections, electronics, personally owned businesses, and other valuable items.

Personal assets can do more than simply help people get loans and count towards net worth. They are also sometimes able to create income for their owners. Bank accounts and savings accounts accrue interest. Holders of real estate are able to lease or rent it out. This brings in rent or lease fees. Individuals who have personal assets should educate themselves in the best practices for managing them so that they are able to increase their total wealth by generating the highest income possible from them.

It is important to keep a careful track of rent or other income obtained from personal assets as the money will be taxable. Income that is not properly reported to the government on the correct tax forms can incur penalties from the Internal Revenue Service.

It is also important to know the value of an individual's personal assets. There are two different methods of learning this. In the first method, individuals examine the item's market value. This is the value for which the asset would sell if a person were to put it straight on the market. Another way to determine the value of these assets is to have a personal asset appraised.

Appraised values can be substantially greater than market values. This is because an appraisal value relies on the possible future price of the item in question. This difference matter significantly, particularly when having an item insured. Individuals generally have to obtain appraised value insurance coverage. This means that they will likely have to pay for a greater amount of insurance.

When properly managed, personal assets can greatly contribute to an individual's personal financial situation. It is also true that these assets can prove to be a liability if they are not well taken care of or managed. Part of managing assets well involves asset allocation.

Financial experts warn against placing all or the majority of personal assets into a single asset type or location. This type of practice causes people to take on additional risk than is prudent. Instead, it is better to spread around an individual's wealth into a variety of different assets so that if one suffers or decreases in value, some of the other assets may offset this by outperforming or increasing in value.

Taking care of personal assets is also an important part of maintaining their value. Individuals can break expensive electronics if they are not careful. Not engaging in proper maintenance for works of art can also lead to their value declining over time.

Portfolio

In the world of business and finance, a portfolio stands for an investment collection that a person or institution holds. People and other entities put together portfolios in order to diversify their holdings to reduce risk to a manageable level. A number of different kinds of risk are mitigated through the acquisition of a few varying types of assets. A portfolio's assets might be comprised of stocks, options, bonds, bank accounts, gold certificates, warrants, futures contracts, real estate, facilities of production, and other assets that tend to hold their value.

Investment portfolios may be constructed in various ways. Financial entities will commonly do their own careful analysis of investments in putting together a portfolio. Individuals might work with the either financial firms or financial advisors that manage portfolios. Alternatively, they could put together a self directed portfolio through working with a self directed online broker such as TD Ameritrade, eTrade, or Scott Trade.

A whole field of portfolio management has arisen to help with the allocation of investment money. This management pertains to determining the types of assets that are appropriate for an individual's risk tolerance and ultimate goals. Choosing the instruments that will comprise a portfolio has much to do with knowing the kinds of instruments to buy and sell, how many of each to obtain, and the time that is most appropriate to purchase or sell them.

Such decisions are rooted in a measurement for the investments' performance. This usually pertains to risk versus return on investments and anticipated returns of the entire portfolio. With portfolio returns, various types of assets are understood to commonly return amounts of differing ranges. Portfolio management has to factor in an individual investor's own precise situation and desired results as well. There are investors who are more fearful of risk than are other investors. These kinds of investors are termed risk averse. Risk averse portfolios are significantly different in their composition than are typical portfolios.

Mutual funds have evolved the act of portfolio management almost to a science. Their fund managers came up with techniques that allow them to prioritize and ideally set their portfolio holdings. This fund management reduces risk and increases returns to maximum levels. Strategies that these managers have created for running portfolios include designing equally weighted portfolios, price weighted portfolios, capitalization weighted portfolios, and optimal portfolios in which the risk adjusted return proves to be the highest possible.

Well diversified portfolios will contain many different asset classes. These will include far more than just stocks, bonds, and mutual funds. They will feature international stocks and bonds to provide diversification away from the U.S. dollar, as well as foreign currencies and hard asset commodities such as real estate investments, and gold and silver holdings.

Portfolio Income

Portfolio income proves to be money that is actually brought in from a group of investments. The portfolio commonly includes all of the various types of investments that an investor owns. These include bonds, stocks, mutual funds, and certificates of deposit. These various financial instruments earn a variety of different types of passive income, such as dividends, interest income, and capital gain distributions. Such portfolio income returns are generated by the holdings of the various investment products in the portfolio.

Portfolio income varies with the types of investments that an investor picks. You as an investor will commonly look at two different factors when assembling a portfolio for portfolio income. These turn out to be the money that the investment itself will produce, which is also known as an investment's return, and the investment's risk level that it contains.

As an example, stocks are frequently deemed to be investments with considerable risk, yet the other side of the risk return equation is that they provide income from a company's dividends, or distribution earnings returned to the shareholders, as well as an increase in the stock price as the stock value gains with time. Certificates of deposit and bonds create interest income that is paid out on the investment that you hold. Still different kinds of investments produce other types of income, although this depends on the characteristics of the investment in question.

To maximize the portfolio income while reducing the amount of risk involved, individuals commonly choose to invest in numerous different kinds of investments. This is known as diversifying your portfolio and portfolio income. This way, you can combine both safer investments that provide lower real returns with riskier investments that offer greater investment returns. Your total collection of investments is the portfolio that makes your portfolio income for you.

This portfolio income is also classified as passive income, or income that does not require you to perform any work in order to make the money. The upfront investment actually creates the income without you having to be actively involved in the money making process. This stands in contrast to incomes that are earned through active involvement, or active income that you must expend both energy and time to create.

The ultimate goal for you with your portfolio income will probably be to build up enough of it that you are capable of living off of only the income that the portfolio generates. Once this point is reached, you would be able to not receive a payroll check any longer. Instead, you would support yourself in retirement from the dividends, interest, and capital gains created by the investments in the form of portfolio income. The best and safest way to do this is to only draw on the portfolio income itself, without drawing down the original principal.

By not touching the investment principal, you allow your portfolio and resulting portfolio income to build up over time. If you do not take out the portfolio income, then the total value of the portfolio will grow faster with time, allowing you to compound your investments for retirement. It is critical to have enough money saved for retirement that you do not need to take out this principal to support yourself. Sufficient portfolio income should be generated to cover the monthly retirement expenses. In this way, you will not be reducing your principal and risking the very real danger of your portfolio running out of money while you are still alive to need it.

Portfolio Manager

Portfolio managers are individuals who invest the assets of a fund. They generally handle either an ETF exchange traded fund, a mutual fund, or a closed end fund. Their responsibility is to carry out the daily trading of the portfolio and to put into practice the fund's investment strategy.

When investors are considering different funds in which to invest, among the most critical elements to think about is the name, reputation, and track record of the portfolio manger. This is especially true if they are involved in active portfolio management as opposed to passive management. Though there are numerous active fund managers in the markets, the track records of historical performances are not encouraging. Only a small minority of them are successful in beating the main market indices.

These managers engage in portfolio management as part of their daily routines. This is the science of making difficult decisions regarding the funds objectives. They must weigh investment mix against objectives, carefully balance the fund risk versus performance, and allocate the assets for the funds customers.

The management of a given portfolio revolves around opportunities, risks, weaknesses and strengths of various categories. These include deciding between equity investments as opposed to debt instruments, international versus domestic securities, and safety as compared to growth. There are numerous trade offs involved in this type of management as a manager makes tough choices in an effort to increase returns to the optimal point for the risk the investors are willing to take.

Passive management is the form of managing a portfolio where the holdings of a fund track an index in the markets. This is most often known as index investing or indexing. Active management is the opposite form. It requires that either one manager, a few managers working together, or even a management team strive to try to outperform the market's return. They try to do this by managing the portfolio actively. They make choices and investment decisions utilizing research on individual securities and positions. Among the different actively managed funds are closed end funds and many mutual funds.

In passive management, the style is to have the holdings of the fund identically reflect the benchmark index. This is the direct opposite of an active style of management where the managers are buying and selling securities in the portfolio according to different investment strategies.

Passive managers and the followers of this particular management type hold with the efficient market hypothesis. This idea says that the markets always reflect and factor in all relevant information all of the time. It believes that picking stocks out individually is a waste of time. Followers of this premise believe that the best method for investing is to put investment funds into index funds. History shows that these funds have performed better than most of the funds which are actively managed.

Active management still has a significant following. It utilizes the human efforts of the management team, co managers, or single portfolio manager to manage the funds portfolio on a daily, weekly, and monthly basis. These active managers work with forecasts, analytical research, and their own personal experiences and judgments to engage in the buying, selling, and holding decisions of the various securities.

The sponsors of these actively managed funds and their investment companies hold that a really good manager can beat the market. This is why they employ professional fund managers to actively handle the portfolio funds. Their goal is to beat those returns of their benchmark. For a large cap stock fund this would mean outperforming the S&P 500 index. Despite the best efforts of a considerable majority of active fund managers, they have not been able to do this successfully.

Preferred Stock

Preferred stock is referred to as preference shares or preferred shares as well. Preferred stock is the name used for a particular equity security which exhibits both characteristics of a stock equity as well as an instrument of debt. Because of this, preferred stocks are commonly deemed to be hybrid types of instruments. In the claims on a company's assets in the event of default or bankruptcy, preferred stocks prove to be higher ranking than mere common stocks, yet subordinated to bonds.

Preferred stocks have a number of interesting properties. They typically come with a dividend that is often fixed. They also enjoy preference versus common stocks where dividend payments are concerned and at any liquidation of the company's assets. A downside to preferred stocks is that they do not include voting rights as do common stock shares. Some preferred stocks offer convertible features that turn them into common shares of stock at a certain time. There are preferred stocks that may be called in early at the wishes of the issuing company. All terms for a preferred stock are listed out specifically in the Certificate of Designation.

Since preferred stocks are somewhat like bonds, the big credit rating companies all rate them for quality of credit. Preferred stocks generally garner lower ratings than do bonds, as the dividends of preferred stocks are not guaranteed as are bonds' interest payments. Preferred stocks are also subordinated to all of the creditors, making them less secure.

Dividends are a key feature of preferred stocks and the main motivating factor in acquiring them. Preferred stocks come with dividend payment preference over other shares. While this does not guarantee that the stated dividends will be paid, the company has to pay such dividends to the preferred share holders before they are allowed to issue any common stock shares' dividends.

These dividends for preferred stocks might be either noncumulative or cumulative. Cumulative preferred stocks mandate that companies who neglect to cover stated dividends up to the full rate must cover them fully at a later date. In each passing dividend time frame, the dividends continue to accumulate. This might be on an annual, semi annual, or quarterly basis.

Dividends that are not paid on time are labeled dividends that have passed. These passed dividends for cumulative stocks are called dividends that are in arrears. If a stock does not possess these cumulative features, then it is called a straight preferred stock, or a noncumulative dividend stock. With these types of non cumulative preferred stocks, the dividends that become passed simply vanish for good if they are not paid on time.

Besides these preferred stock features, they have various other rights. Some types of preferred shares do include a particular group of voting rights for the approval of unusual events like the ability to issue and sell extra shares, to approve the company to be sold, or even to choose the board of directors' members. In general, preferred stocks do not have voting rights. Many preferred shares also come with a liquidation value that states what sum of money was put into the issuing corporation as the shares became issued.

Profit Sharing Plan

Profit Sharing Plans are not all the same. These plans can come in a range of different formats. Many times they are utilized as a supplement to another kind of retirement account. These defined contribution plans prove to be a significant benefit with tax advantages for a number of American employees.

The reason that employers establish these types of plans is to provide valuable employees with another method of compensation. This particular one permits the employees who participate to receive a portion of company earnings from a trustee. Individuals who have the benefit of a profit sharing account will enjoy contributions made by their employers to their personal plan account. They can then invest these funds and increase them tax free. Maximum individual employer contributions per year are limited to $53,000.

There is a caveat to many of the retirement plans that are employer sponsored. They typically require the employees to become vested in the plan over a period of pre-defined years in which they participate. It might be the employees gain 20% vesting per year over five years. While Money Purchase Plans set up a pre-arranged percentage of yearly earnings which become contributed to the accounts, profit sharing works differently. These plans and their contributions are based on the profitability of the company.

The rules that are typical of these defined contribution plans apply to profit sharing as well. Withdrawals can not be taken before the account owner reaches 59 ½ years of age. If they do take distributions earlier than this, the withdrawals will be fully taxed like personal income. They will also have the standard 10% early withdrawal penalty assessed against them.

The money from profit sharing plans is commonly invested by the trustee administrators into one of several investments. These include variable annuities, mutual funds, company stock, or life insurance. In rare cases with specific job scenarios, the individual employee may be allowed to manage the investment vehicles within the profit sharing account.

Rollovers have a specific set of rules that govern them with profit sharing accounts. The only money from these accounts that can be rolled over is that which has become fully vested. It is important to understand completely the schedule for vesting before account holders think about moving retirement funds to another qualified type of account. The IRS has no unusual restrictions on transferring vested profit sharing account funds. The plan administrator will have to mail out specifically detailed explanations to the account holder of how this can be done without incurring any taxes or penalties.

This is important because if the distribution is not properly rolled over, then the disbursed funds may be treated by the IRS as an early withdrawal. In this case, they will be taxed as ordinary income and suffer the 10% penalties for being taken out ahead of minimum retirement age. This is why transfers such as these should be done as direct rollovers in lieu of indirect rollovers whenever possible. Withholding requirements apply to indirect rollovers besides the danger of experiencing penalties for accidental early distribution.

Plan providers determine what specific investment choices an account owner may pursue with the money from their profit sharing plan. Much of the time, account holders do not have the ability to determine the investments that their profit sharing money participates in at all. The IRS allows investments for these funds that include individuals stocks, government and corporate bonds, mutual funds, options, and exchange traded funds shares.

While these choices may be available to a profit sharing plan account owner, investing in physical gold bullion and the other precious metals is not. Gold ETFs and gold mining company stock shares may be an alternative option for those who wish to diversify away from dollar based assets.

Required Minimum Distribution (RMD)

The Required Minimum Distribution is a concept that pertains to retirement accounts and IRS rules which govern their distributions. Many individuals are not aware that they can not simply choose to hold retirement money in their retirement vehicle forever. They must begin accepting withdrawals from their traditional IRA, SEP IRA, Simple IRA, or other type of retirement plan and account after they turn age 70 ½. The notable exception to this rule is for Roth IRAs, which do not mandate disbursements while the owner is still alive.

The required minimum distribution is literally the minimum legal dollar amount that account holders have to take out of the retirement account every year. Naturally most people choose to withdraw a larger amount than this required minimum. Withdrawals that are received must be detailed in the individuals' taxable income. The exception to this is for any income that had been previously taxed as with Roth IRA contributions or any earnings which accrued on a tax free basis. This relates to distributions from Roth IRA accounts.

Figuring out the actual amount of the RMD is not so easy. The simplest way to do it is to work with the IRS published Uniform Lifetime Table. In this method, people figure their RMD in any given year by taking the balance from the end of the prior calendar year and dividing this amount by a distribution period taken from the Uniform Lifetime Table. There is also a different table to be utilized if the owner of the account's spouse is the only beneficiary and he or she is at least ten years younger than the owner.

The IRS provides worksheets on their website to help account holders figure up the mandated minimum amount. They also provide several tables to help with this. As mentioned, the Uniform Lifetime Table is for every IRA account owner who is figuring up his or her own withdrawal. The Joint Life and Last Survivor Expectancy Table is for those whose spouse is at least ten years younger and who is the only beneficiary.

The initial date for the first RMD on an IRA is figured out by taking the April 1st of the year that comes after the calendar year in which the account holder turns 70 ½. With a 401(k), 403(b), profit sharing plan, or similar defined contribution plan, either this same April 1st deadline applies or the April 1st that follows the calendar year in which the owner actually retires.

The individual turns 70 ½ on the calendar date which falls 6 months following his or her 70th birthday. The plan terms themselves govern whether the individuals can wait until the year in which they actually retire to take the initial RMD. Other plans will require distributions begin on the April 1st following the year of turning 70 ½ whether or not the person has retired.

Once account holders have received the first RMD, they must take their subsequent ones on or before December 31st. It is possible to avoid having the first and second RMD's included in a single tax year. In the year individuals turn 70 ½ they can simply go ahead and take that first RMD by the end of the year to avoid the double distribution taxation in one calendar year.

People who do not take their full minimum required distribution will suffer an IRS penalty. Any amount which they do not take as the law requires will suffer a 50% excise tax that will be levied on it. This failure to take the RMD must be reported on a Form 5329, Additional Taxes on Qualified Plans.

Reverse Annuity Mortgage

A reverse annuity mortgage has several different names. Industry insiders call them reverse mortgages or home conversion loans. The government and finance companies created them to assist retirees who find themselves in a condition of being rich in assets but poor in cash. There has become a greater need for this type of product as more and more individuals find themselves increasingly retiring with only the significant asset of their house.

A greater number of individuals now only receive social security payments after they retire. This amounts to less than $20,000 for an individual or perhaps around $30,000 for married couples. It means that there usually will be a massive need for more money coming in during the retirement years. This gave rise to the concept of the reverse annuity mortgage.

This specially tailored reverse annuity mortgage allows homeowners to sell part or all of their house now but to remain in it until they die. It provides money that retirees are able to utilize for a variety of needs. This could be to supplement the monthly income. It might also be used for medical expenses, long term care, home maintenance, or even the overseas trip of a lifetime.

The way these reverse mortgages work is fairly straight forward. Finance companies provide a set dollar amount of money. Homeowners can receive monthly income as with the reverse annuity mortgage. They might also get a lump sum amount from the option for home equity conversion. The borrowers do repay the loan principle along with interest. What makes these vehicles unique is that there is no physical repaying of the funds. The debt accrues to be paid back after the owners sell the house. This is usually after the retirees have passed away or gone into a permanent care facility.

When retirees choose the annuity option, they utilize the funds from the house to purchase a lump sum annuity. This pays out every month so that they can count on monthly payments that continue until they die. It provides tremendous security for struggling retirees who have only their house to help out their situations.

Scams are a significant and real concern with a reverse annuity mortgage. Retirees are often taken advantage of and cheated. There are companies that charge even thousands of dollars in exchange for information which the HUD provides for free. They disguise these fees under their estate planning service contracts. Fees can amount to from six to ten percent of the full amount the retirees borrow. This can cost even tens of thousands of dollars depending on the reverse mortgage amount. HUD has advised reverse mortgage lenders to not work with such companies.

Other companies are using reverse mortgages as a way for retirees to pay for a significant purchase such as insurance or annuities which they sell. They often hide unethical and exorbitant fees or unfair terms in their contracts. Some lenders will include share appreciation or share equity terms. This can ravage the retirees' equity position and not give them any benefits in return.

Individuals are able to protect themselves from such scams in the reverse mortgage field. The simplest and most effective means is to work with a reverse annuity mortgage counselor that the HUD has approved. They will evaluate the retiree's scenario as well as the contracts on a reverse mortgage. These specialists will find any possible problems and make it clear what needs to be changed or avoided.

Rollover IRA

An IRA is the acronym for Individual Retirement Account. These accounts represent a form of government-approved and -created savings account for retirement. They have several advantages, the main one of which is the significant tax breaks they receive in tax deferment. This makes them the optimal way to put cash aside towards eventual retirement. It is important to know that IRAs are not investments. Instead they are more like the basket in which individuals maintain their mutual funds, stocks, bonds, and other assets. When one retirement account is transferred to another one, this is known as a Rollover IRA.

Generally people open such a Rollover IRA themselves. There are also a few types which small business owners and the self employed can open. Among the various types of Individual Retirement Accounts in existence are the Roth IRAs, traditional IRAs, SEP IRAs, and SIMPLE IRAs. Not all of these can be accessed by every individual in the U.S. This is to say that every one of them has specific eligibility requirements which revolve around the type of employment and income level. What they do all have in common is the caps on the amount individuals are allowed to contribute every year. They also mostly share steep penalties for withdrawing funds ahead of the government set age of retirement.

The greatest benefit to these accounts lies in their ability for all of the assets within the plan to gain in value while not being taxed by the U.S. Federal government. This means that all income generated by capital gains, dividends, and interest will compound every year with no tax bite. Taxes on the majority of these forms of IRAs only become due as the owners take qualified (or unqualified with a penalty) distributions. There are two different forms of this. With the majority of the IRAs, individuals are able to commit pre-taxed dollars to the account. With Roth IRAs, the dollars are after-taxed, but then no additional taxes on them will be required upon withdrawals at retirement. Using the Rollover IRA concept, individuals can switch from one type of IRA to another.

The Internal Revenue Service strictly limits how much money people can put into such accounts. The majority of individuals who are less than 50 are not permitted to contribute over $5,500 each year as of 2016. These limits become higher once the holders attain an age greater than 50. They call this "catch up contributions," and the limits are typically raised by $1,000 to $1,500 more in this decade immediately before holders reach retirement age.

Practically all individuals are allowed to make contributions each year to a traditional form of IRA. So long as either the holder or spouse earns taxable income and is less than 70 and a half years old, they can participate.

The various kinds of IRAs are important to understand. A ROTH IRA does not provide tax deductions on contributions. There are also income restrictions which in 2016 amounted to under $184,000 for married filing jointly families or $117,000 for single heads of households or those who are married filing separately and not living with their spouses.

Both SEP and SIMPLE IRAs apply to only small business owners and the self employed. Only employers who claim fewer than 100 employees can set up these SIMPLE IRA accounts. Any individual who possesses freelancing income or who owns a business can open an SEP IRA.

While individuals can always withdraw their contributions (and even earnings) at any point once they have deposited them to their IRAs, there are penalties if they are less than 59 and ½ years old. The penalty is an extra 10 percent above the that-year tax bracket of the individuals who take distributions early. The government's point is to discourage people from utilizing their retirement accounts like ATM machines or credit cards.

Roth IRA

A Roth IRA is a particular type of Individual Retirement Account. These Roth IRA's prove to be special retirement plans that are given favorable tax treatment. The tax laws of the United States permit tax reductions on restricted amount savings for retirement accounts.

Roth IRA's are different from other IRA's in several ways. Among the chief of these is that tax breaks are not given on monies that are put into the plan and account with a Roth IRA. Instead, these tax breaks are given out on the money and its investment gains when they are taken out of the account at retirement. This chief appeal of Roth IRA's is that they provide completely tax free income at retirement.

Other Roth IRA benefits over traditional forms of IRA's exist as well. The restrictions placed on the kinds of investments that they are allowed to contain are fewer. You can turn them into gold IRA's and annuity account IRA's. Roth IRA's can also contain all of the usual forms of investments that IRA's contain, such as mutual funds, stocks, bonds, and certificates of deposit. More unusual investments such as real estate, mortgage notes, derivatives, and even franchises are allowed to be purchased with Roth IRA's. These investment choices do depend on the capability and allowance of the Roth IRA trustee, or firm with which the plan is set up. Roth IRA's also permit you to make un-penalized withdrawals of all direct contributions that you make, after the first five years of the account have and plan have passed, which is certainly not the case with traditional IRA's.

These distributions, or withdrawals, are not taxed because they are taxed before the contributions are made. The penalties are waived for principal, as well as interest and earnings in the account, if the distributions are for purchasing a house or for disability or retirement withdrawal uses. If there is not a justified reason for the distribution, then the account earnings and income made above contributions will be taxed.

All IRA's contain specific limits on the dollar amount of contributions that the government permits. This amount changes per year, and is set through the year 2011 now. Presently, you can put $5,000 per year into Roth IRA's. There are income restrictions that govern whether you are allowed to make this full contribution as well. Individuals who make less than $106,000 are permitted to make full Roth IRA contributions, and those who make under $121,000 may make a partial contribution. Married couples who file together are allowed to earn less than $167,000 to make their full contribution to the Roth IRA, while those who make under $177,000 can do a partial contribution.

Roth IRA conversions from traditional IRA's have been allowed by the IRA in the past, although with certain income restrictions. Beginning in 2010, this policy changed. Now the IRS permits any persons, regardless of how much money that they make, to convert their traditional IRA's into Roth IRA's.

SARSEP

SARSEP is an acronym that means Salary Reduction Simplified Employee Pension Plan. The government offered this advantageous retirement vehicle to those small businesses which possessed fewer than 26 employees. With this SARSEP, employees receive their own SEP IRA account in their specific individual name. They and their employers can both make contributions to the accounts.

These accounts are interesting primarily because they were stopped in January of 1997. In 1996, Congress passed the Small Business Protection Act which eliminated the SARSEP accounts. They became replaced by Simple IRA plans on a going forward basis. Those SARSEPs that already existed have been grandfathered in to the system. They continue to function unchanged as before.

Employees may make contributions to their accounts by using pre tax reductions from their salaries. Employers also may contribute as they so desire. Their total is limited to the lesser amount of either $53,000 or 25% of the total salary of the employee. Employees are limited to an annual contribution amount of $18,000 (or $24,000 if they are 50 years or older).

Besides this, net profits limit the total amount of all contributions that can be made to the account. These may not be greater than 18.6% of the company's net profits for 2016 per the SEP IRA self employed rules. All of this means that SARSEPs are SEP IRA collections held by an employer. The individual accounts of employees are governed by the IRS rules for SEP IRAs.

The IRS does allow transfers or rollovers to be made from SARSEPs. Employees can do these without incurring tax penalties by moving the money to another account that is also qualified. Both plans in question have to permit rollovers from other retirement savings vehicles. Individuals may also choose to move a part of the account value or the whole account balance in an SEP rollover.

Anyone who receives distributions before reaching the minimum retirement age of 59 ½ will be penalized with the 10% early withdrawal penalty. To avoid these problems by accident, direct rollovers make more sense than indirect rollovers. With an indirect rollover, there are requirements for withholding. Accidental early distributions still incur penalties if the rollover is not completed within 60 days.

SARSEP accounts are unusual retirement vehicles. They may hold precious metals and a variety of other non traditional investments within them. These include individual stocks and bonds, mutual funds, options, ETFs, CDs, real estate holdings, and physical precious metals bullion. This makes these SEPs more versatile than the traditional and other types of IRAs. They permit investment choices from regular IRAs as well as hard commodities and land. This makes SARSEPs one of the only ways to possess actual gold, silver, palladium, or platinum in a retirement account.

Per the IRS, legally these types of accounts can hold all of these different kinds of assets. The only exception to this ability comes down to the particular contract of the individual accounts. The SEP IRA custodian may not make all of these types of investments available to their account holders.

Also choices for such investments can be limited by the written employer account agreement. This is why it is critical to read these agreements and to talk with the account custodian before making investment choices. In the event that physical precious metals are not permitted by the custodian or employer, paper gold is still an option. This includes Gold ETFs or gold miner ETF shares, as well as gold mining company stocks.

Self Directed IRA

Self directed IRAs prove to be special kinds of individual retirement accounts. They are different from traditional IRAs because they provide the account holder with a significantly greater variety of investment choices and control over decisions on the account. With these types of IRAs, the owner or an investment advisor makes a variety of investment decisions. They then deliver these instructions to an IRA custodian who executes them.

Federal law allows these types of IRAs to invest in a tremendous range of investment vehicles. It is IRS section 408 that restricts the few categories that are not allowed. The IRS forbids investments of IRA funds in life insurance and collectibles such as rugs, art, gems, etc. It does allow a wide range of investment choices that cover most anything else.

Self directed IRAs may purchase real estate, mortgages and trust deeds, energy investments, gold and other precious metals in bullion form, privately held stock, privately owned LLCs and Limited Partnerships, and corporate debt or promissory notes. When accounts such as these are opened primarily to purchase precious metals bullion, they are typically known by the name of their primary metal in which they invest.

These Precious Metals IRAs can be called Gold IRAs, Silver IRAs, Platinum IRAs, and Palladium IRAs. Such self directed IRAs can even purchase franchises such as Subway or Timothy Horton. All of these different investment choices allow for superior and broad based asset diversification of investors' retirement funds.

These types of IRAs also provide all of the usual benefits which are commonly associated with Traditional IRAs. Money saved in these plans is contributed on a tax free or tax deferred basis. No taxes will be paid on either the money deposited, or the gains made on these investments within the account, until they are withdrawn at retirement or under early withdrawal rules and limitations. Self directed IRAs are still subject to the same yearly maximum contribution limits of $5,500 in 2016. They allow for larger contributions of $6,500 to be made as catch up once the account holders reach age 50.

Early withdrawals from these IRAs as with traditional ones are penalized. It is often more advantageous to take a loan against the value of the IRA rather than suffer the financial consequences of early withdrawal. When loans are taken, there is no penalty. A repayment plan is established to put the borrowed funds back in the account in installments. Loans can be approved for a variety of expenses, such as home purchase, educational needs, or health care related expenses.

When an actual early withdrawal is taken, two penalties are assessed. First the money in the account is taxed as ordinarily earned income. Next a 10% penalty is levied by the IRS on all monies which the owner early withdraws.

These types of IRAs do have some limitations. The custodian must physically hold all assets in the account. This means that the account owners are not allowed to keep their real estate or mortgage deeds, stock certificates, or precious metals bullion at home in a safe. There have been offers made by some companies to help investors become their own IRA custodian by forming a special LLC company. This is a gray area which the IRS has not yet come down on with a hard ruling. In the future, they are likely to rule that investors absolutely can not be a custodian for their own gold, silver, platinum, or palladium bullion using either a safe deposit box or a home based safe.

The IRS requires that owners of these accounts begin taking distributions no later than at age 70. They can start withdrawing them as retirement funds at 59 ½ if they wish to begin using the money earlier.

SEP IRA

SEP IRAs are special simplified employee pensions that permit employers to contribute money to the retirement plans of their employees. If individuals are self employed, they may also set up and fund one of these accounts for their own benefit. These plans compare favorably to the more popular and utilized 401(k) plan. SEPs offer greater contribution amount limits. They are also much less complicated to establish and maintain than are the 401(k)s.

Any type of employer is allowed to create an SEP IRA. This means that businesses which are not incorporated, partnerships, and sole proprietorships can all work with and utilize them. Even self employed individuals who are employed elsewhere as well (with retirement plans at their other workplace) can make their own SEP.

SEP IRAs offer several advantages to owners and contributors. They provide significant tax benefits for employees and employers. Employer contributions give tax deductions to the employer during the tax year in which they make the contribution. Self employed individuals also can take this tax deduction for themselves. SEPs are also popular because they do not require any annual paperwork to be filed with the IRS. The paperwork that creates these accounts also offers the plus of being simple and minimal.

Individuals can make contributions for SEP IRAs in the year after the contribution applies. Deadlines for these contributions may also be stretched to the tax return due date. As far as establishing these accounts goes, deadlines are for the tax return due date and any extension that the IRS grants on the taxes.

In general, these accounts have to be opened and all contributions should be made by the April 15th that comes after the year in which the income was attained. Any taxpayers who take an extension on their tax returns to October 15th would receive a similar grace period for opening and funding the SEP IRA.

The contribution amounts for SEPs are quite flexible. No set percentage has to be contributed as with some of the rival retirement accounts like

Keoghs. One could contribute nothing or as much as 25% of his or her income for the year (on as high as a $265,000 income amount). The full contribution for a single individual is not allowed to be greater than $53,000 in the year 2016. This amount contrasts with the typical standard IRA contribution limits of $5,500 for the year 2016.

The SEP limits are also substantially higher than the contribution limits on 401(k)s that come in at $18,000 for 2016 or at $24,000 for those who are at least 50 years old. SEPs do not have any provisions for catch up, as with other forms of IRAs or 401(k)s. Thanks to the higher contribution limits for every given year, this does not usually present a problem for those who are behind on their retirement accounts and want to put in more.

Employers are required to treat all employee contributions equally. This means that they must give the same contribution percentage for each employee who has made at least $600 in the year, who is 21 years or older, and who has worked for the company minimally three out of five prior years.

The only point where contributions to SEP IRAs get complicated centers on maximum contribution amounts. The 25% of income limit mentioned earlier is not figured out of gross revenue, but from net profits. Besides this, deductions on the half of self employment tax have to be first taken off of the net profit number before the limit for maximum contributions can be accurately determined off of the net profits.

Simple IRA

Among the stable of various types of IRAs American savers for retirement can take advantage of is a less common plan called the SIMPLE IRA. These kinds are a combination of traditional IRAs and employer offered plans like 401(k)s. The word SIMPLE in this case is actually an acronym that stands for Savings Incentive Match Plan for Employees. This is the most common name for the employer offered tax deferred retirement savings account.

SIMPLE IRAs were created to help smaller employers who have 100 or less employees. The idea was for them to offer their workers retirement plans. The IRS knew that the bigger packages of benefits all too often involved long and difficult opening procedures with mountains of complicated paperwork. Smaller employers simply did not have the time or resource capacity to complete and maintain these types of plans.

Among the advantages of SIMPLE IRAs is that they are not governed by ERISA, the Employee Retirement Income Security Act. This means that they are able to sidestep substantial expenses and significant amounts of paperwork in establishing them. The contributions to these kinds of IRA accounts are also fairly straightforward. Employers must make specific minimum amount contributions to the accounts of the employees.

They can accomplish this by establishing a match program at a minimum of 3% of their employee contributions. Alternatively they might set a 2% of his or her salary flat rate and offer it to every employee who participates.

When employees become part of a company SIMPLE plan, they are basically establishing a traditional IRA via their employing company. A significant disadvantage to these types of IRAs centers on their lower contribution limits. These are less than comparable 401(k) plans or other plans which employers sponsor. The limits amount to $12,500 for a single year in tax years 2015 and 2016.

Rolling over from these types of IRAs is also more complicated. They can not be started without a waiting period first being observed. Once employees start their participation with the plans, they can not do a rollover for generally two years on from their participation dates. The only exception to this rule pertains to transfers between SIMPLE IRAs.

These can be done at any time since they are considered to be a tax free transfer from one trustee to another. In the even of any other type of transfer within the two years waiting period, these are deemed as distributions by the IRS. While most penalties for tax deferred plans are set at 10% withdrawal penalties, these particular IRAs carry a more punishing 25% withdrawal tax penalty.

After the conclusion of the two year time frame, individuals may then move their funds from the SIMPLE plan to a different kind of IRA. The only restriction is that they can not move them to a Roth IRA which is funded with pre-taxed dollars. The current SIMPLE plan as well as the new plan must also allow for the transfer to occur.

As with any kind of retirement plan, early withdrawal penalties apply. If any withdrawals occur before the official retirement age of 59 ½ is attained, the early withdrawal penalties of up to 25% will be assessed against the account withdrawals.

When rollovers are done, direct rollovers are much preferred to indirect rollovers. If account holders pursue indirect rollovers there are tax withholding requirements. It is also possible that the account owner will inadvertently fail to complete the transfer in time or at all and then suffer from the substantial early withdrawal tax penalties of up to 25%.

Social Security

Social Security in the United States refers to the federal government's OASDI Old Age, Survivors, and Disability Insurance program. President Franklin Roosevelt created the first such program and signed the Social Security Act legislation in 1935. The present day law has been amended to include other social insurance and social welfare schemes.

The Social Security program is mostly bankrolled using payroll taxes which are referred to as the FICA Federal Insurance Contributions Act tax. The other legislation on it pertains to self employed people. SECA Self Employed Contributions Act Tax collects their contributions. The Internal Revenue Service collects all of these tax deposits and delivers them to the two Social Security Trust Funds. These are the Federal Disability Insurance Trust Fund and the Federal Old Age and Survivors Insurance Trust Fund. All income paid by salaries to a maximum amount set by law contributes to the payroll tax for these programs. Income that people earn above this limit does not incur additional taxes for the programs. This maximum level of taxable earnings in 2016 amounted to $118,500.

The program provides a basis for economic security for 59 million Americans who are retired, disabled, or the family members of those who are deceased or disabled workers. This number amounts to about one in six Americans who receive money from the program. Of this amount approximately 39 million beneficiaries are retired while the rest are survivors of deceased or disabled workers or disabled people themselves. Around 163 million individual Americans pay these taxes so that the others can receive their monthly benefits. This amounts to around a quarter of families collecting income from the programs.

Social Security proves to be a program based on a pay as you go system. Today's workers contribute taxes into the program so that money can go directly out in the form of monthly income to the recipients. This makes it different from prefunded company pension plans. Prefunded programs collect money in advance of retirement benefits being paid. This way it can be distributed to the workers of today when they retire.

Both workers and employers make contributions to the program. Workers give 6.2 percent of income up to the cap. Employers similarly pay an amount that is matching to arrive at the joint contribution of 12.4 percent of all earnings. Those persons who are self employed must pay for both employer and employee share.

Social Security's finances have a bleak outlook. The Office of the Chief Actuary of Social Security comes up with a "best estimate" on when the fund will run out of money to pay benefits. If Congress makes no changes to the law, then in 2020 the benefits spending will actually surpass the revenues for payroll taxes along with the interest on the funds' securities.

At this point, the fund will start cashing in its Treasury securities it obtained as IOU's for loaning money to other branches of the Federal government. In order for the government to pay these IOU's, they will have to obtain money from one or more of a few different sources. Other spending will have to decrease, taxes will have to rise, or the Treasury will have to borrow additional money by selling more securities. This last choice would increase the already high Federal debt.

By 2034, all the assets of the trust fund would have been completely exhausted. This means that all Treasuries the fund has would have been redeemed. By this point, the combined workers and employers taxes would be enough to cover 79 percent of currently promised benefits to recipients. The last year of the 75 years projection shows that by 2089, the payroll taxes would be sufficient to cover around 74 percent of currently promised benefits.

Solo 401(k) Plan

Solo 401(k) plans function much as their standard 401(k) plan cousins do, but display some important differences. These retirement savings plan vehicles for the self employed are also called One Participant 401(k)s, Self Employed 401(k)s, Individual 401(k)s, and Uni-Ks.

These particular 401(k)s provide business owners and spouses who do not have any employees beyond themselves with the ability to be a part of a 401(k) type of tax deferred plan. The plans are fairly new. Congress unveiled them as part of their 2001 Economic Growth and Tax Relief Reconciliation Act. At the time, these became the first specially tailored employer sponsored retirement plans intended for the self employed. Before their introduction, these self employed persons could only rely on such plans as IRAs, Keogh Plans, or Profit Sharing Plans.

These Solo 401(k)s possess practically identical requirements and rules as do the normal 401(k) plans. There are two important exceptions to this. The owner and the business do not find themselves governed by the expensive and complicated requirements of the ERISA Employee Retirement Income Security Act. Besides this, the company is not permitted to employ additional employees who are full time workers contributing 1,000 hours or more each year to the business.

Contributions also have their own particular rules with these Solo plans. The account owner is also both the employee and employer. For the 2016 tax year, employee contributions are limited to $18,000 (or $24,000 per year in the case of those who are fifty years of age or older). Other contributions can be put in as employer contributions. Whichever type a business owning participant wants to call these contributions, the limit for both employee and employer contributions may not be more than $53,000 for a given year.

One benefit that holders of these Solo 401(k) plans enjoy is that they do not have to employ a custodian as with IRAs. Instead they can work with practically any financial institution or bank as their account trustee. Assuming that the trustee will handle it, these plans are able to invest in a wide range of alternative asset types. This includes mutual funds, individual bonds and stocks, ETFs, CDs, real estate, life insurance, S corporations, and precious metals bullion such as gold or silver. Solo Plans are almost unique in their ability to invest in life insurance, which even the self directed IRA plans are not enabled to do.

This all makes the Solo 401(k)s practically unrivalled in their capability to provide retirement plans with low costs, that are easy to make transactions in, with great flexibility, and with generous contribution limits all at once. The downsides to the Solo 401(k) are two. Most workers are not allowed to participate with them. They also need a great deal of paperwork and account maintenance when measured up against numerous other types of retirement plans.

Rollovers are easy to do with these Solo plans. They are able to receive such transfers from other kinds of accounts and IRAs. Account holders may also transfer or roll them over to another kind of retirement account. It is important to check with the rules of an individual's particular plan, as some plans do not accept rollovers from the Solo 401(k)s. Besides this, there are Solo 401(k)s that specifically do not permit rollovers.

Business owners should take care when setting up these types of accounts. Rolling over these types of retirement vehicles will not incur any IRS tax penalties, so long as they are done according to the IRS rules and regulations. An individual has 60 days to finish the procedure and may only engage in it one time per year. Failing to abide by these rules will incur regular income taxes plus the 10% penalty for early withdrawals, unless the individual is older than the 59 ½ years retirement age.

Stock Broker

Stock brokers are professionals who are both licensed and registered with the Financial Industry Regulatory Authority or FINRA. In general, stockbrokers work for a broker dealer or a stock brokerage firm. Stock brokers are not to be confused with financial advisors or financial planners, who perform many different services for their clients.

Stock brokers have a primary responsibility. Their job is to purchase and sell stocks, bonds, mutual funds, and other related investments on behalf of their clients. These clients can be retail investor individuals or institutional clients. Institutions as clients refer to not for profit companies, universities and colleges, foundations, and other similar groups.

Stock brokers trade stocks for their clients over a stock exchange or sometimes an over the counter market. Among the larger and better known stock exchanges are the New York Stock Exchange and NASDAQ. They are compensated for these trades with commissions or fees that the trader pays. These fees range widely from one type of stock broker to another. Online stock brokers offer the lowest commissions to their clients. These types of brokers usually charge under $15 per trade.

There are a variety of names for stock brokers in the industry. These various titles refer to different licenses the brokers may hold, the various services they deliver to their clients, and the kinds of securities which they trade. Stockbroker is an older designation for these individuals who are now more commonly referred to as brokers, reps, registered reps, or financial advisors.

Not all of these titles refer to exactly the same type of professional. The scope of a financial advisor or financial planner is generally much broader than that of a stock broker. A stock broker would primarily handle the trades in and out of given securities. Financial advisors and planners look at the entire picture of a person's investments and future goals to come up with a comprehensive investment and financial plan for the individual.

The requirements to become a stock broker vary. In the U.S., these professionals usually need to hold a bachelor's degree. The brokerage firms are preferably looking for applicants who have a business degree in a subject such as finance, economics, accounting, or a related field. Those applicants who possess master's degrees in business or finance receive preferential hiring treatment. Because they are in greater demand, they are able to command higher salaries than applicants who only hold bachelor's degrees.

Once a stockbroker candidate is selected, they must be sponsored by the brokerage that hired them. They can only take the exams required by the stock market industry if they have the sponsorship of such a brokerage firm. There are a variety of exams that are available to stock broker candidates. American stock brokers have to take and successfully pass the Series 7 exam, as well as the Series 63 exam or the Series 66 exam. Once they have completed such exams, they can be registered with the Financial Industry Regulatory Authority. At this point, the candidate is officially a registered representative, or stockbroker.

In the past, a stock broker was a professional that only wealthy investors and individuals could afford. They were able to access stocks and other investments through these brokers. Minimum account sizes kept out smaller investors generally.

Thanks to the Internet, access to the markets broadened considerably. Discount brokerage firms and discount stock brokers proliferated. These allow for individual investors to trade stocks and other investments for low and reasonable fees with much smaller minimum account sizes. They do not offer personal advice to their clients. Thanks to these changes that technology empowered, most any individual is able to invest in the markets today.

Stocks

Stocks are financial instruments that are issued by publicly traded corporations. These shares of stocks prove to be the tiniest portion of ownership that you can acquire in a company. Even by owning a single share of a company's stock you are a small part owner of the firm.

Owning shares of stock gives you the privilege of voting for the underlying company's board of directors, along with other critical issues that the company is considering. Should a company decide to distribute earnings to share holders as dividends, then you will get a portion of them.

With the ownership of stock, your liability in the company is only limited to the value of your shares. This means that should a company lose a lawsuit and be forced to pay an enormous fine or judgment, then you can not be made to contribute to it. The company's creditors also can not pursue you if the company runs into financial trouble and goes bankrupt.

Two different types of stock shares exist. These are common shares and preferred shares. The vast majority of shares that are issued are common stock shares. These are the shares that members of the public hold most of the time. They come with full voting rights and also the possibility of receiving dividends that the company pays out.

Preferred stocks come with fewer voting rights but give preferential treatment for dividend payment Preferred stock issues are paid out before common share dividends. Companies that offer preferred stock typically pay dividends on both classes of shares anyway. Preferred stocks also have a higher claim on the assets of a company if it fails.

Liquidity is a feature of stocks that should always be considered. Common stock shares are almost always more liquid than are preferred shares. Large companies offer the greatest amount of liquidity in the trading of their stocks. Because of the depth of the stock markets, you are able to purchase and sell the shares of practically all companies that are publicly traded at any time that the exchanges are working.

When you purchase a stock, you are looking for two different kinds of gains.

Cash flow or passive income with stocks comes from the dividends that they declare and pay out. Capital gains appreciation is realized when you buy a stock at a lower price than the price that you get when you later sell it. While cash flow dividends are smaller payments that are realized on a generally quarterly basis, capital gains turn out to be larger one time returns made when you sell the underlying stock shares investment. At this point, you would no longer own the stock and you would have to purchase another stock in order to work towards cash flow gains from dividends, as well as other possible capital gains.

Supplemental Security Income

Supplemental Security Income refers to the emergency measure benefits for retirement that are provided to working Americans by the government to help cushion their golden years. For those retirees whose regular social security check amount is insufficient to provide for their basic retirement needs, the government set up an additional sum of money provided monthly that is called Supplemental Security Income, also commonly known by its acronym as SSI.

The same Social Security Administration which delivers the regular Social Security checks also maintains the SSI program. They created it to provide additional help for the financial needs of some retirees who possess limited income and few resources for retirement. This monthly benefit which SSI provides for those who are at least 65 years old is also delivered to those retirees who are either blind or in some meaningful way disabled. This commonly creates an income overlap between the traditional social security retirement checks and the SSA disability benefits which many people receive. Yet those recipients who fully meet all eligibility requirements are able to receive money out of each program.

It is important to keep in mind that they are a few critical differences from one program to the next. Obtaining normal Social Security benefits is only a matter of having worked for a minimum number of years (either an individual or the spouse) so that coverage is obtained under the rules of the program. With Supplemental Security Income though, there is no past work required to become eligible for monthly payouts. The funding for the SSI program is derived from another source than that which provides for the regular Social Security benefit checks. In truth, even a different federal authorization grants the money from the general taxation that helps to provide for the payments of SSI.

In fact, being eligible for SSI often has a connection with various other state and/or Federal benefits and programs. In the majority of states, those SSI beneficiaries are also eligible for medical assistance from the state-provided Medicaid programs. These will help to pay for the costs of any necessary hospital visits and stays, prescription drugs, doctor bills, and other related health care costs. States have the discretion to add on supplemental amounts to the SSI payments as they wish. They will commonly employ identical financial and income criterion in ascertaining who is eligible and who is ineligible. In almost all of the states, SSI recipients also qualify for and receive food assistance.

There are several financial resource tests which determine the eligibility for Supplemental Security Income benefits. The financial assets limitation is $3,000 for couples and $2,000 for individuals. There can be some exceptions made in calculating financial assets. The most critical is that an individual does not have to include the value of the home in which he or she lives, the primary vehicle for transportation, or the personal effects and other household goods. Other limited assets include life insurance and burial funds which individuals can own. Scholarships and grants for educational costs and retroactive SSI benefit and Social Security payments are also excluded.

A few other assets also will not be counted for the purposes of coming up with SSI asset limitations. These include those properties which are critical for self-sufficiency and also money that has been saved in a particular Individual Development Account. Earned income tax credit payments, relocation assistance payments, federal tax refunds, and crime victim's assistance payments similarly will not be counted for from nine months to 12 months after they are received. Some trusts can also be exempted from this asset limitation calculation.

Tax Exempt Income

Tax Exempt Status means that certain transactions or earnings in the form of income will not be taxed at either the local, state, or even federal, (or a happy combination of all three) level. As taxpayers earn their income or sell some of their assets to realize a gain before the end of a given tax year, then they create a tax liability for themselves with the government. Tax deductions should never be confused with tax exemptions, since these deductions only lower the residents' tax liabilities.

Tax exempt items are those which are entirely excluded from any forms of tax computations. Items which are tax exempt income might be reportable on the individuals' (or otherwise business or not for profit organization entities') tax returns only as information. It is important to note that these exempt items are not included in the tax calculations.

A common example of tax exempt income is municipal bonds which pay interest. Such bonds are those which cities and states issue in order to generate money for particular projects or general operations. For those taxpayers who gain interest income off of such municipals which are sold from the state in which they reside, this income becomes exempted from both state and federal taxes for them.

In these cases, taxpayers will be given a 1099-INT form to be utilized for all investment interest which they earned throughout the year. All tax-exempt interest will be reported on box eight of the tax form. Such interest earnings will only be reported for the purposes of providing information. It would not be covered in the calculations for personal income taxes. In other cases, interest earnings are fully taxable events.

There are some kinds of capital gains which can be classified as tax exempt income as well. For instance, these capital gains could be offset against other cases of capital losses in the same taxable year. As an example, investors who make $10,000 in capital gains and who also realize $5,000 in capital losses at the same time on a different asset or investment will only pay their taxes on the $5,000 net capital gains which remain after subtracting the capital losses from the capital gains in the same taxable year.

In many cases, when there are significant capital losses, these can be "carried forward" into the future to offset any capital gains for those coming years. American Federal tax codes also permit taxpayers to take a part of their capital gains from home sales and exclude them from federal taxes. This is permissible up to a specific and pre-set dollar amount. The rule became set up in order for those homeowners who sell their homes to be able to protect these gains from taxes so that they can help to fund their future retirements.

Another factor which affects tax exempt income is a calculation known as AMT, or alternative minimum tax. This secondary tax calculation can be required on some individual tax returns. Alternative Minimum Tax considers some previously ruled out as tax exempt items and puts it back into the personal tax calculation. As an example, income from municipal bonds is put back into the mix when using the AMT calculations. Taxpayers are often required to use an AMT calculation on their original tax returns so that they can be made to pay the higher amount of tax from the larger tax liability.

Tax Sheltered Annuities 403(b)

Tax sheltered annuities are retirement savings programs and vehicles that the Internal Revenue Service allows for under the 403(b) section of their tax code. They were created for the benefit of employees who work for churches, educational institutions, and specific not for profit agencies.

They offer the advantage of permitting employees who are eligible to participate to contribute nearly all of their annual income towards retirement savings and investments in the plan. As an example of the generous limits with these particular plans, employers who choose to contribute can put in as much as $53,000 as of 2016 for any single tax year.

This supplemental program for retirement savings gives participating individuals a variety of ways in which they can choose to contribute funds. They may invest on an after tax basis, as with a Roth plan. They may also choose to contribute using funds that are pre-taxed. They can also opt to use a combination of the two methods. These plans and their participating contributions are entirely voluntary. Employees generally make the majority of these contributions as there is not always an employer match involved with them.

A variety of employees of eligible organizations may participate in these tax sheltered annuity plans. Employees of public schools, universities, and state colleges are allowed to participate. Many employees of churches are also allowed to become involved. Those who work for the school systems run by Indian tribes and their governments may participate. Not for profit 501(c)(3) churches' and organizations' ministers are included in them, as are ministers who are self employed who serve as part of a tax exempt organization. Chaplains are also usually qualified to participate.

There are several good reasons to become involved with these tax sheltered annuity plans. With automatic payroll deductions, it is a simple and relatively painless means of building up extra savings which individuals will require to increase their after retirement income.

They can get involved in a low cost program that is flexible enough to offer a good selection of investment choices. People can make contributions on a Roth after tax basis, a pre tax basis, or a combination of the two. Finally these plans are portable, meaning the owners can take their retirement vehicles with them when they move to a different job or another not for profit organization.

Thanks to these plans and vehicles, account holders are able to invest tax money that would otherwise go to the IRS. They can move money between the various funds in the plans without suffering from capital gains taxes or additional fees. This gives these TSA pre tax accounts a greater return than a taxable account would enjoy if it earned similar returns. For any individuals who use these account vehicles as Roth after tax accounts, all qualified distributions at retirement will be enjoyed completely tax free.

Money from these accounts can not be taken out without penalties until the individual reaches the government mandated minimum retirement age of 59 ½. They must begin taking distributions by the time they turn 70. An exception to the minimum retirement age is for individuals who stop working for their not for profit company before they reach retirement age. In this case, they are allowed to go ahead and begin receiving distributions without having to pay the extra 10% early withdrawal penalty tax. Only any taxes that were due for monies which had been contributed as pre tax dollars would apply in this particular case.

Tax-Deferred

Tax deferred money and status pertains to earnings on investments. This includes dividends, interest, and capital gains which are allowed to accumulate without taxes paid until the owner withdraws the earnings and gains. The two most popular kinds of these deferred investments are found in IRAs and tax deferred annuities. Growth that is tax deferred permits gains to be compounded instead of having taxes paid on them.

Investors gain in two different ways from having taxes deferred on their investment returns. The first method is through growth on investments which is tax free. Instead of having to pay taxes on the present returns of the investment, the taxes are not paid until a later time. This allows the investment to increase without setbacks.

The second method from tax deferral pertains to investments which are entered in pre-retirement accumulation phases. At this point, the earnings and taxes on them are generally significantly higher than earnings will be when the owners retire. This means that withdrawals drawn out of deferred accounts typically happen after individuals are bringing in less taxable income. The end result is that their tax rate is at a lower level than the one the IRS applies with they are still working.

There are a number of qualified and approved tax deferred vehicles available today. Probably the most common and popular is the 401(k). Employers provide these plans as a company benefit to help their employees to increase their retirement savings.

Third party administrators act to deduct contributions from employee payrolls and help manage the plans. The employees then get to choose from several options in which to invest their tax deferred savings. These include company stock, mutual funds, or some fixed rate choices. All gains made in these accounts do no add to the taxable earnings of the employees participating. These contributions they make to the 401(k) and other qualified accounts like most IRAs come from pre-taxed dollars. This means that the employee's taxable income amount becomes reduced.

When the employees surpass the minimum 59.5 retirement age, they are able to take distributions from these plans. The taxes they pay are only those which apply on their earnings as they are received. So investors who may earn enough to pay 33% tax bracket while employed will likely pay as little as 10% to 15% taxes on distributions they take from their 401(k) plans at retirement that they have along with their any other income from interest, social security, or pensions.

401(k)s typically involved employer dollar matching programs that inspire employees to set aside a greater amount of their earnings in order to increase the size of their retirement nest egg. In putting the money off to the future, they will pay fewer taxes in the end.

It is important to understand the difference between tax deferred and non tax deferred retirement vehicles. Some retirement investment accounts are not tax deferred. The owners pay the taxes on the earnings before they contribute them to the accounts. The advantage to this is that all interest, dividends, and capital gains grow without any other taxes being owed on them when they are taken out as distributions at retirement age. One beloved insurance product that works this way is an annuity.

Retirement plans like traditional IRAs have annual contribution limits of $5,500 per year as of 2016. Annuities do not come with such annual restriction levels. Employees can contribute even millions of dollars per year to them if they wish.

The earnings made in these insurance backed products grow without having taxes taken out of them even at retirement. This means that any and all earnings in these account compound fully from the second year of the annuity contract. So long as the gains earned are taken out after the employee reaches 59.5, there will not be any taxes or early withdrawal penalties of 10% levied against the earnings in these pre-taxed contribution accounts.

Tenure Annuity

A Tenure Annuity is a type of reverse mortgage monthly payment plan. This program delivers cash payments that are consistent to the home owning seniors for an unlimited amount of time until they pass away or move out of the house. The agreement remains in force up to the point that both spouses leave the house that backs the loan. Tenure payment amounts are usually fixed based on the primary borrower's age.

Such a tenure annuity can be crucial for those seniors who do not have much monthly income or savings. They likely still want to take advantage of activities which provide an active and enjoyable retirement. The monthly payments from these tenure annuities can be used at the discretion of the borrower. They might use them to supplement benefits from social security. Medical costs can be paid with them. Seniors can work to pay down debts using the funds or to improve, renovate, or repair their home. They can even put them to use for leisure activities and travel opportunities.

Financial planners often advise seniors to increase their retirement income streams using a tenure annuity. This is because the income from private pensions and/or social security is often insufficient to meet their expenses and desires. There are many benefits to these plans. One of the most important is that they deliver a guaranteed and predictable monthly payment that boosts other income sources.

A tenure annuity has numerous other advantages. The money will be provided for as long as the borrowers live in the house, whether this is for from a few months to several decades. The arrangement is fully covered and backed by the FHA Federal Housing Administration. The borrowers continue to enjoy complete and unrestricted use of their house that is tied to the reverse mortgage. There is no burden of monthly mortgage payments as with a traditional mortgage loan. Finally, there are no additional collateral requirements besides the house itself.

One of the valuable characteristics of a tenure annuity is that the debt builds up against the home slowly. The equity for the future payments remains in the house until it is needed. This means that the estate of the borrowers will be significantly greater if they die early than for a senior who simply took out the maximum cash value in the reverse mortgage.

A tenure annuity also provides flexibility for the senior borrower. These participants are able to modify the transaction by simply paying a minor $20 fee to the loan servicer.

As an example, a borrower who determines he or she will not require the monthly tenure payment amount for some time can change the house's unused equity over to a credit line. The credit line increases in size every month as the payment amounts of the annuity build up in the line. In a case where the opposite is true, seniors who require bigger payment amounts are able to switch over into the term annuity from the line of credit.

Another useful feature of the tenure annuities is that they protect the value of the property from declining. Whether the borrower chooses the monthly payments, the credit line, or switches back and forth, the protection remains the same. Thanks to the FHA coverage of the reverse mortgage, the borrower is not liable for any declines in the value of the home.

Term Life Insurance

Term life insurance is a form of life insurance. It offers coverage for a preset and limited amount of time that is called the relevant term. The coverage provided is a fixed rate of payment coverage. Once the term expires, the individual's coverage at the rate of the premiums that were charged before are not assured any more.

The client will be forced to drop their term life insurance coverage or to get a different coverage with varying payments and terms. Should the person who is insured die within the term, the death benefit amounts are paid out to the insured person's beneficiary. This term life insurance proves to be the most affordable means of buying a major dollar value of death benefit coverage based on the premium cost charged.

Term life insurance turns out to be the first type of life insurance created, and it stands in contrast to permanent forms of life insurance like universal life, whole life, and variable universal life. These coverage types promise an individual pre set premiums that can not go up for the person's entire life. People do not usually employ term insurance for strategies involving charitable giving or their needs for estate planning. Instead, they are thinking about a need to replace an income if a person passes away on his or her family unexpectedly.

A great number of the permanent life insurance policies also offer the advantage of increasing in value during the person's contract. This cash value can then be withdrawn when certain conditions are met by the policy holder. Generally, withdrawing these cash amounts closes out the policy. Beneficiaries of permanent life insurance products get the insurance policy face value but not the cash value upon the holder's death. Because of this, financial advisers will suggest that people purchase term life insurance for their insurance needs and then invest the money saved over permanent products in retirement accounts that provide tax deferred contributions and investment gains, like 401k's and IRA's.

Like with the majority of insurance policies, term life insurance pays out claims for the insured, assuming that the contract is current and the premiums are paid as due. Assuming that a claim is not filed, the premium is not given back to the policy holder. This makes term life insurance like home owners' insurance policies that pay claims if a home becomes destroyed or damaged as a result of fire, or like car insurance policies that pay drivers if they have a car accident. Premiums are not refunded when the product is no longer required. Because of this, term life insurance like these other products only provides risk protection.

Thrift Savings Plan

The Thrift Savings Plan represents a government created retirement savings vehicle. In 1986, Congress passed the Federal Employee Retirement System Act. This plan was established for the benefit of retired or present employees in the civil service of the federal government.

In 2001, Congress expanded the TSP so that it would include the members of the armed forces with the National Defense Authorization Act. This extended participation beyond the original civilian employees. Armed forces members were allowed to enroll beginning on October 9th of 2001.

The Thrift Savings Plan was set up to be a defined contribution plan. The goal behind its creation was to provide the federal government employees with similar retirement savings types of benefits as private sector workers had. Employees in the private sector already enjoyed these retirement savings opportunities via the available 401(k) plans. With every payroll check, plan contributions to both the 401(k) and TSP are deducted automatically.

These TSPs include a variety of different funds. Participants can choose from and invest in six different types. Among these are the government security fund, the common stock fund, the fixed income fund, the international stock fund, the small cap stock fund, and the life cycle fund.

The government security TSP fund is specifically managed by the Federal Retirement Thrift Investment Board itself. This fund's management purchases U.S. government guaranteed Treasury securities that are not marketable. Because of this conservative and safe strategy, the G Fund does not lose money. Its returns are also lower as a result of this low risk.

The common stock fund is one of the index funds that track a particular benchmark. In the case of this C fund, it invests in a stock index fund which mirrors the composition of the Standard and Poor 500 Index (S&P 500). This means it buys an index based on the various stocks of the 500 medium to larger sized American corporations. Its goal is to replicate the S&P 500s annual performance.

With the fixed income fund, it also tracks a benchmark index. This F fund's goal is to match the Barclays Capital US Aggregate Bond Index's performance. This broad based index was established to represent the bond market in the United States. As such it returns earnings commiserate with American corporate bond performances.

As the name implies, the international stock fund buys prominent stocks of international companies. It also follows a benchmark index. This particular I fund tracks the MSCI Europe, Australasia, Far East Index also known as the EAFE. Its returns are made up of gains or losses from the stock prices, income from dividends, and fluctuations in the comparative currency valuations. Regardless of what is happening in international markets, this fund and the fixed income, common stock, and small cap stock funds are always fully invested.

The small cap stock fund buys the index fund of stocks which follows the Dow Jones US Completion Total Stock Market Index. This S Fund earnings come from both dividend income received and any losses or gains in the prices of the underlying stock.

An interesting combination is the life cycle fund. These are managed to invest in the five different TSP funds. They professionally determine the allocations and percentages in each based on the retirement time frame set by the owner. There are L2020, 2030, 2040, and 2050 versions which assume that within a few years of those dates the owner will be looking to retire and be more conservatively invested.

TSP benefits are several. Government agencies are able to match employee contributions. They also have an agency automatic contribution option. Employees can make catch up contributions when they reach a certain age. These funds feature low, affordable expense ratios. All contributions made to these plans are not taxed until the point where the money is withdrawn at retirement.

Traditional IRA

The Traditional IRA is the most common type of the various individual retirement accounts available to savers for retirement. Besides this type of IRA, there are also SEP IRAs, Roth IRAs, and Self Directed IRAs. Each of these types of accounts has at least a few features in common with the original and still most popular plain IRA.

These accounts are all particularly designed to help save, grow, and fund individuals' retirements. They all permit investors to trade a variety of securities, such as stocks, mutual funds, ETFs, and bonds. Different from other kinds of brokerage and investment accounts, IRAs most importantly offer account holders tax benefits. The main difference between traditional IRAs and Roth IRAs centers on the way taxes are paid or deferred by the IRS rules.

With a Roth IRA, owners pay taxes on contributions now. All gains that account holders make in the account then accrue tax free for the entire life of the retirement savings vehicle. The traditional forms of IRAs give holders the advantage of tax deferred contributions. This means that they will not have to pay any taxes on money contributed until they withdraw them later on at retirement time. All gains that they earn in the account over the life of the IRA will be taxable at the time they withdraw them.

With all of these types of IRAs, the annual contribution limits remain the same. For tax year 2016, this amount is $5,500 for individual contributions or $11,000 for married individuals filing jointly. Catch up contributions are also the same in these various kinds of IRAs. When people reach age 50, they can make additional contributions amounting to $1,000 each year for an individual or $2,000 for married people filing jointly.

This means that instead of adding $5,500 individually to the IRA for the year, an individual could contribute $6,500 per year once he or she turns 50. Similarly married individuals would be allowed to add $13,000 per year instead of $11,000 annually once they both reach age 50.

Traditional IRAs do not feature any income limits while Roth IRAs do have these. People can be disqualified from making investments in their Roth

IRAs if they earn too much money any given tax year. Single filers are only allowed to make less than $110,000 each year. Above this income, the contribution amount which the IRS allows tapers down until the income reaches $125,000.

Once this income limit is reached, a Roth IRA contribution is disallowed for the tax year. With married filing jointly, the income maximum is higher. With under $173,000 earned for the year, the full $13,000 maximum contribution is permitted. This amount tapers off as the earnings rise to $183,000. Beyond these earnings, two individuals who are married are not allowed to utilize the Roth IRA in that particular tax year.

IRAs are different from 401(k)s, the other popular retirement savings vehicle, in several critical ways. Traditional and the other forms of IRAs can only be set up and maintained by an individual acting on his or her own behalf. 401(k)s are retirement accounts that employers set up on behalf of their employees. Many employers make partially matching contributions to their employees' 401(k) accounts.

IRAs also commonly offer superior choices in different investment possibilities than do the more limited 401(k) plans. Self directed IRAs are allowed to invest in most any type of investment that is not considered to be a collectible item. This means that Self Directed IRAs are allowed to invest in franchises, real estate, precious metals, mortgages, energy, and other alternative investment ideas.

Treasuries

Treasuries refer to United States Treasury Securities. These Treasuries are United States government debt that is actually issued and sold by the Department of the Treasury via the Bureau of Public Debt. The U.S. government uses its Treasury securities to finance the enormous and rising debt of the Federal government. In common and investor vernacular, these treasury securities are commonly simply called Treasuries.

Four different kinds of treasury securities exist. These are Treasury notes, Treasury bills, Treasury bonds, and TIPS, or Treasury Inflation Protected Securities. Other types of treasury securities are not marketed. These are comprised of savings bonds, Government Account Series debt given to trust funds that the government manages, and SLGS, or State and Local Government Series. The former marketable Treasury securities prove to be extremely liquid and also are traded significantly on the secondary market. The latter mentioned non marketable Treasury securities are only sold to subscribers. They may not be transferred back and forth via market sales.

The vast majority of U.S. Treasuries are actually held by other countries. As of January 2010, the top five largest holders of American Treasuries turn out to be China with $889 billion, Japan with $765.4 billion, the combined oil exporting nations with $218.4 billion, the United Kingdom with $206 billion, and Brazil with $169.1 billion. China and Japan combined hold an enormous $1.6 trillion worth of U.S. Treasuries.

These and other foreign countries have become such a large component of U.S. Treasuries debt purchases that many economists have grown afraid. They fear that since foreign nations now account for such a great percentage of U.S. Treasuries that should they decide to stop purchasing them, the U.S. debt and economy might simply collapse. The possibility that this is true has caused many observers to believe that the two economies of the United States and China are inextricably linked. Both countries are afraid of what would happen if the Chinese slowed their purchases of U.S. Treasuries. When Hillary Clinton, the U.S. Secretary of State, visited China earlier in 2010, she insisted that Beijing monetary authorities keep buying United States Treasuries. Her argument centered on the hope that this will pump the American economy back up, which would stimulate Chinese goods' imports back home.

China has demonstrated its frustration over the possible decline in value of its U.S. Treasuries holdings too. The Chinese Premier Wen Jia Bao has expressed concern and a warning that the Chinese holdings of U.S. Treasuries could be downgraded and devalued if Washington can not get its runaway debt under controlled.

Treasury Bills

Treasury Bills prove to be among the largest category of United States issued Treasuries. They are also called T-Bills for short. Treasury Bills have maturities of a year or less. They never pay investors interest before they mature, making them somewhat like zero coupon bonds. The government instead sells Treasury Bills at a face value discount, which causes there to be a positive yield to maturity. Numerous economists and ratings agency consider Treasury bills to be the lowest risk investments that American and foreign investors can purchase.

T-bills come issued with varying maturity dates. These typical forms of weekly Treasuries can have four week maturity dates, thirteen week maturity dates, twenty-six week maturity dates, and fifty-two week maturity dates. Every week, the government runs single price auctions for its Treasury bills. The quantity of thirteen week and twenty-six week Treasury bills available for purchase at auction are actually announced every Thursday. They are then offered on Monday and issued on the next Thursday.

Four week T-bill quantities get announced Mondays for next day auctions. The bills become issued on Thursday. Fifty-two week bills become announced only on the fourth Thursday, to be auctioned the following Tuesday and issued that Thursday. Associated purchase orders have to be received before 11 AM on Monday auctions at Treasury Direct. Minimum purchases for these T-bills are a reasonable $100, marked down from the former $1,000 minimum. The Treasury redeems T-bills that mature every Thursday. The biggest buyers of T-bills prove to be financial institutions such as banks, and primary dealers in particular. These Treasuries in their individual issue all get one of a kind CUSIP numbers.

Sometimes the Treasury cash balances are lower than usual. At these times, the Treasury often opts to sell CMB's, or cash management bills. They sell these in much the same way as T-bills, at auction with a discount. Their main difference lies in their irregular amounts and shorter terms of fewer than twenty-one days. They also possess different week days for auction, issue, and maturity. As these CMB's mature on the identical week day as typical T-bills, commonly Thursdays, they are termed on cycle.

When they instead reach maturity on another day, they are known as off cycle.

Treasury bills are regularly sold on the secondary market too. Here, they are both quoted and sold via annual discount percentages, known as a basis. The secondary market trades these T-bills heavily.

The Treasury has modernized its means of offering T-bills to investors recently. Treasury Direct is their means of selling T-bills over the Internet, so that funds can be taken out and then deposited straight to the individuals' bank accounts. This permits investors to make better rates of interest on their savings than with simple bank account interest.

Trust Fund

A trust fund proves to be a specific kind of legal entity. It contains property or cash which it holds to benefit another group, individual, or organization. Numerous different kinds of trusts exist. They are governed by almost as many provisions that determine how they work. Every trust fund involves three critical parties. These are the grantor, the beneficiary, and the trustee.

A grantor is the individual responsible for creating the trust fund. Grantors can do this with a variety of assets. They might give stocks, bonds, cash, mutual funds, real estate, private businesses, art, or other items of value to the fund. They also determine the terms by which the trustee will manage the fund.

Beneficiaries are the individuals who receive the benefit of the fund. The grantor sets it up on their behalf. The assets the grantor places inside of the trust fund are not the property of the beneficiary. The trustee oversees them so that the financial gain benefits this individual according to the rules laid out by the grantor at the time he or she establishes it.

Trustees are the managers of these funds. They could be an institution like a the trust department of a bank, an individual, or a number of trusted advisors. Their job is to make sure that the fund fulfills its duties spelled out by the governing law in the trust documents. Trustees typically receive small management fees. The trustee could manage the assets directly if the trust specifies this. In other cases, trustees have to pick out investment advisors who are qualified to manage money.

Trust funds come to life under the rules of the state legislature where the trust originates. Different states offer advantages to certain types of trusts. This depends on what the grantor wants to do by establishing the fund. This is why attorneys help to draft the trust documents to make sure they are correct and most advantageous. As an example, there are states which allow perpetual trusts that can continue forever. Other states make these illegal because they do now want to enfranchise a class of future generations who receive substantial wealth for which they did not work.

Special clauses may be inserted into these trusts. Among the most heavily used is the spendthrift provision. This keeps the beneficiary from accessing the fund assets to pay debts. It also allows parents to ensure that any irresponsible children they have do not find themselves destitute or homeless despite poor decisions they may make.

Trust funds provide a large number of benefits. They receive special protection from creditors. They ensure that family members follow wills after the grantor passes away. These trusts also help estates to avoid as many estate taxes as possible so that wealth can reach a greater number of generations.

Trusts can be an ideal way to ensure the continuity of a business. Sometimes business owners wish to protect a company and their employees after they die. They might still wish for the profits to benefit their heirs. In this case, the trustee would oversee the management of the business while the heirs reaped the financial rewards but could not break up or ruin the company through mismanagement.

Trusts can also be used with life insurance to transfer significant amounts of money which will benefit the heirs. A small trust could purchase a grantor life insurance. When the grantor dies, the insurance money funds the trust. The trustee will then buy investments and give the rents, interest, and dividends to the beneficiaries.

Trustee

Trustee refers to either a firm or an individual who possesses assets or real estate property on behalf of a third party individual, group, or organization. Trustees are often appointed to perform a great range of functions. These could be for charities, bankruptcies, trust funds, pension plans, or retirement plans.

As the name implies, these individuals or firms are entrusted with taking the optimal decisions which are in the primary interest of the beneficiary. Because of this sacred trust, these are often considered to be fiduciary responsibilities for the beneficiary or beneficiaries of the trust in question. This means that they are legally bound and obligated to perform these duties to the very best of their capabilities.

The granting of the prestigious title and responsibilities of trustee comes in the form of a legal title bestowed by a trust. Trusts themselves prove to be legal arrangements which two willingly consenting parties agree to make. Because of the fiduciary nature of the trustee role in any trust which the individual or organization oversees for the beneficiary or beneficiaries, they must lay aside any and all hopes of individual gain or personal agendas so that they can perform the best actions on behalf of the trust.

In other words, the trustee carries the full responsibility for correctly and optimally managing both the financial assets and real estate types of property which the trust itself possesses. There will always be duties particular to the specific details of the trust which the trustees must perform. The differing types of assets will naturally dictate the activities which the trustees must engage in for the beneficiaries' common good.

It helps to consider a real world example to more fully understand the somewhat complex concept. When trusts are made up of a range of real estate properties, the trustees will be responsible for properly overseeing the maintenance and handling of the particular pieces of property. In other cases, a trust might be comprised of different investments such as stocks, mutual funds, and bond holdings in a stock brokerage firm account. The trustees in this case will have to properly oversee and mange as necessary the account or accounts for the beneficiaries.

Trustees also have certain guidelines to which they must adhere in general. Among these common responsibilities which pertain no matter what the particulars of the trust agreement may actually be, the assets must be at all times kept under the direct control of the trustees so that they are securely accounted for each and every day. Trustees also must fully grasp the often unique terms of their particular trust, the responsibilities they are incurring by taking on the role, and the wishes of the applicable beneficiaries. Assets which may be invested must be considered productive so that they will benefit the beneficiary or beneficiaries in the future.

Besides this, the trustees have to both understand and properly interpret the trust arrangement so that they can effectively administer the assets' distribution to the correct parties and/or beneficiaries. This includes the duties of compiling all appropriate records for the trust. Among these there will be tax returns which they must file and pay and statements that they must produce and deliver to the beneficiaries. As such, the trustees will be expected to maintain regular communication with all beneficiaries so that they remain informed of the value of related accounts and any taxes which will become due.

In the end, all trustees have the distinction of being the ultimate decision makers regarding every trust-related matter. They must make such decisions according to the particular provisions contained within their unique trust arrangement and contract. It also means that if beneficiaries have questions regarding a decision which the trustee is preparing to take, that they must first obtain answers for these beneficiaries before they engage in the given decision.

U.S. Treasury Bonds

U.S. Treasury bonds are bonds that the United States government issues so that it is capable of paying for Federal government projects. When a person or business purchases a Treasury bond, they are actually loaning the Federal government money. Like with all loans, the principal is paid back along with a set rate of interest.

Treasury bonds carry the full faith and credit guarantee of the United States government. This translates to them having very low risk, as the government is always able to print extra money to repay the loan. Another benefit to U.S. Treasury bonds lies in their being tax exempt from local and state taxes. You would still have to pay Federal taxes on all money that you make in interest.

The primary market is where the government markets its Treasury bonds through auctions. You might also buy them on the secondary market using a broker. While the government does not charge fees for partaking in their auctions, brokers likely will expect to receive fees for selling you a U.S. Treasury bond. The Treasury bonds are marketable securities since you are able to sell or buy them once you have obtained them initially. They are considered to be extremely liquid too, since the secondary market for them is very active. The prices for Treasury bonds both at auction and via the secondary market are set by their interest rates. Today's Treasury bonds can not be called back by the government before maturity, which means that you continue to receive interest until they mature.

Treasury bonds are not without their downsides. Should interest rates rise while you have a Treasury bond, then your money will be making lower interest than it might in another investment. If the interest rates were to increase, then the bond's resale price would also go down. Inflation that goes up also cuts into the Treasury bonds' interest that they pay. With practically no risk of the U.S. government defaulting on these bonds, Treasury bonds pay a low return on investment, so higher inflation rates will wipe out all or most of the interest profits as they lower the real worth of the principal and interest repayments.

If you are interested in becoming involved in government auctions to buy the Treasury bonds straight from the Federal Reserve Bank, then you can do so. Simply open a Treasury Direct Account. The government does not charge fees for such an account until it has in excess of $100,000. For these larger accounts, they collect tiny maintenance fees.

Besides Treasury bonds, the government also sells two other kinds of securities. These are Treasury bills and Treasury notes. Treasury bonds are distinguished from these other two types by their length of time till maturity. Treasury bonds do not mature until from twenty years to thirty years elapse. They do make coupon payments of principal and interest in every six month period, like with Treasury notes. Thirty years maturities prove to be more common than do the twenty year maturities with these Treasury bonds.

UniCredit Bulbank

UniCredit Bulbank proves to be the biggest bank in the Republic of Bulgaria. Until 1994, this state-controlled and -operated bank bore the name of the Bulgarian Foreign Trade Bank or BFTB. It was in 2007 that the UniCredit Bulbank became formed when Bulbank, Hebros Bank, and Biochim merged together as individual subsidiaries of UniCredit Group from Italy.

Bulgarian Foreign Trade Bank first arose in 1964 in its headquarters of Sofia, Bulgaria. The at the time completely state-owned and -founded bank held an initial paid in capital of 40 million Bulgarian leva when it opened. This proved to be a large sum of capital in this day and age. At the time under the heyday of the communists in Bulgaria it specialized in foreign finance and foreign trade payments.

The bank realized that to effectively pursue foreign trade and finance, it needed several well placed good international branches. The bank then began to open important representative offices in London, Vienna, and Frankfurt throughout the subsequent decades. In 2015, the operation boasted substantially greater assets amounting to nearly 9 billion Euros and 2015 era equity of nearly 13 billion Euros.

Once Communism collapsed in Bulgaria during the successful national coup in 1989, the country established the Bank Consolidation Company in 1991 to operate the state- controlled banking sector and to help with the eventual privatizing of the various national Bulgarian banks. BCC owned 98 percent of the share capital of Bulbank at the time. It became the first Bulgarian bank operation to change over to international SWIFT codes. This helped it to massively improve its transaction reliability and operational performance as a direct result.

The bank's eventual privatization from 1998 to 2000 saw UniCredito Italiano gain control of 93 percent of the capital shares while German based re-insurance giant Allianz obtained another five percent of the remaining shares. Bulbank then sold its majority stakes in Corporate Commercial Bank and minor stakes in United Bulgarian Bank and HypoVereinsbank Bulgaria.

Bulbank has continuously worked on the merger of operations and branches between the old Bulbank offices and Hebros Bank and HVB Bank Biochim since UniCredit made the decision to merge the HVB Group back in 2005. The group was renamed UniCredit Bulbank officially at this point.

The same Chief Executive Officer has overseen the company's massive successes since the year 2001. This towering figure in Bulgarian banking and finance is Mr. Levon Hampartzoumian. He heads UniCredit Bulbank still as of end of 2016 in its second decade of existence in the present foreign owned-form of the financial institution.

Part of the leading in Bulgaria success that UniCredit Bulbank has consistently enjoyed in recent decades stems from the wide range of clientele they effectively serve. They offer bank checking, current, and savings accounts, insurance and investment products, land and home mortgages, and financing and credit for individual clients, private banking customers, small businesses, large corporate clients, other financial institutions, and even Bulgarian government and other public institutions as well.

UniCredit Bulbank is not only by far and away the largest bank in Bulgaria by branches, deposits, and assets; it is also a heavily award-winning financial institution. In 2016, it received the honors of "Bank of the Year" from the Association Bank of the Year and "Best Bank for 2016" from Global Finance Magazine. It is known as the "Best Digital Bank in Bulgaria for 2016" per Global Finance Magazine. Focus Economics ranks it as the "Most Precise Overall Economic Forecast for Bulgaria." Forbes Magazine labeled it the "Most Innovative Bank in Bulgaria". It received the "Best Bank in Bulgaria" designations from EMEA Finance Magazine and K10's Kapital Newspaper annual ranking. Global Finance Magazine called UniCredit Bulbank the "Best Trade Finance Bank in Bulgaria" in 2016, as did Euromoney Magazine as well.

Vested Rights

Vested Rights refers simply to rights that cannot be taken away. In finance, they refer specifically to one of several topics. The most common pertains to employer-provided retirement benefits or stock incentives. They describe the non-forfeitable rights on either employer contributions to the qualified retirement plan or pension plan account or to stock incentives provided as a valuable incentive by the employer. Such vesting will give the employee tangible rights to a portion of the employer-owned assets over time.

This provides a substantial incentive for the employee to deliver his or her best efforts to the company and to stay with it a long time as well. Vesting schedules are always determined by the employing firm. They specify when the employee will then acquire full ownership of the funds, stock, or other asset in question. In general, such non-forfeitable rights will accrue on a time schedule based on the number of years the employee has been with the company.

The amount of time for vested rights to be earned varies from one plan document to the next. It always helps to consider a good example to better understand somewhat complicated topics such as these. An employee could get 100 restricted shares of stock in the firm for which he works as a portion of the yearly bonus. The goal would be to find a way to keep the valuable employee at the firm. The company can do this by spelling out a several year vesting schedule for the stock shares.

For example, it would be common for the stock to vest at the rate of 25 shares (as in 25 percent) per year starting on the completion of the second year. This means that after year three, the employee will be fully vested in 50 shares (50 percent), while after the fourth he or she will have vesting in 75 shares (75 percent), and finally at the end of the fifth year, he or she will entirely own the 100 shares of bonus stock (100 percent vesting). Should the employee part ways with the company at the end of the fourth year, then he or she would have 75 shares of the stock while the remaining 25 would forfeit back to the firm.

There are other benefits where the vested rights are effective immediately. As an example, all employees always gain 100 percent vesting in their own contributions from their salaries to their retirement plans and SIMPLE employer contributions and SEP employer contributions. Generally, any employer contributions to the employee 401(k) plan will also immediately vest. There are other scenarios where this money only vests after a few years on what is called a cliff vesting schedule. This provides the employee ownership of 100 percent of all employer contributions only after completing a pre-determined number of years with the firm. There are also graded vesting schedule options to firms, which mean that the employee gains ownership of a set percentage of all employer contributions made very year. With many traditional pension plans, they will have either a three to seven years long graded vesting schedule, or alternatively a simpler five year cliff vesting schedule built in to their policy.

Becoming one hundred percent vested in an employer retirement plan and employer provided contributions are not a carte blanch to draw out the money on demand though. The rules of the plan will still govern in this regard. They will likely insist that any employees attain legal retirement age before they are allowed to engage in withdrawals without any penalties being assessed.

Wealth

Wealth proves to be the abundant possession of material things or other resources that are considered to be valuable. People, areas, communities, or nations who control these assets are said to be wealthy. The word for wealth comes from the old English word 'Weal' and 'th', which means 'the conditions of well-being'.

The ideas of wealth have great importance for every part of the study of economics. This is particularly the case with development economics. Since the definition of wealth often depends on the situation in which you use it, no universally accepted definition for wealth exists. Different individuals have expressed a number of varying ideas of wealth in differing scenarios. Stating the concept of wealth often involves ethics and moral issues, because the accumulation of wealth is viewed by many people as the highest goal.

Wealth is not evenly distributed throughout the world. In the year 2000, world wealth estimates ranged around $125 trillion. The citizens of Europe, North America, and a few high income Asian countries have ninety percent of all of this wealth. Besides this shocking statistic, only one percent of all adults on earth possess forty percent of the planet's wealth. This number declines to thirty-two percent when wealth is calculated according to purchasing power parity, or equivalency of what it buys from one country to the next.

Wealth and richness are two separate words that are used interchangeably. They mean slightly different things. Wealth describes gathering up resources, whether they are common or abundant. Richness relates to having such resources in abundance. Wealthy countries and people possess many more resources than do poor ones. The word richness is similarly employed to describe peoples' basic needs being fulfilled through sharing the collective abundance. Wealth's opposite proves to be destitution, while richness' opposite is known as poverty.

It is a concept that requires a social contract of ownership to be set up and enforced. Ideas of wealth are actually relative. They range from not only one society and people to another, but even between varying regions or areas of the same society or nation. As an example, having ten thousand dollars throughout all of the United States does not make a person among the richest in any area of the country. But this amount in desperately poor developing nations would represent a huge quantity of wealth.

The idea of wealth changes in different times too. Thanks to the progress of science and machines that save labor, even the poorest in America today benefit from a higher standard of living than the wealthy used to enjoy not so long ago. Assuming this trend continues, then the wealthiest people's standard of living today will be considered poor in the future.

Other Financial Books by Thomas Herold

The Money Deception - What Banks & Governments Don't Want You to Know

High Credit Score Secrets - The Smart Raise And Repair Guide to Excellent Credit

Other Books in the Herold Financial IQ Series

99 Financial Terms Every Beginner, Entrepreneur & Business Should Know

Personal Finance Terms

Real Estate Terms

Bank & Banking Terms

Corporate Finance Terms

Investment Terms

Economics Terms

Retirement Terms

Stock Trading Terms

Accounting Terms

Debt & Bankruptcy Terms

Mortgage Terms

Small Business Terms

Wall Street Terms

Laws & Regulations

Financial Acronyms

www.ingramcontent.com/pod-product-compliance
Lightning Source LLC
Chambersburg PA
CBHW071414210326
41597CB00020B/3500